D0771165

Whitaker on Watercolor

IN A PROVENCE MARKET. 19¾″ x 29″

Whitaker on Watercolor

Frederic Whitaker, N.A.

 Reinhold Publishing Corporation/New York

CONTENTS

Color Plates

DESIGNED BY MYRON HALL III

TYPE SET BY HOWARD O. BULLARD, INC.

PRINTED AND BOUND BY THE COMET PRESS, INC.

6   *CHURCH IN MORELIA*

INTRODUCTION

There are two kinds of students of painting: hobby painters and those who seriously plan to make art their life work. Hobby painters usually want to achieve results quickly. Many want to skip such fundamentals as drawing and the study of composition. Their attitude is understandable, for usually their painting time is limited by other duties which to them are more important. But more dedicated students do not insist upon immediate results. They realize that to become a good artist entails long study and practice, and they are prepared to give the time, energy, and concentration needed. Obviously, a book directed to only one group would not satisfy the other.

What I have attempted in this book is to cover the whole field of watercolor, beginning with simple fundamentals and ranging through more advanced technical procedures. There are also chapters on the problems of exhibiting and the history of watercolor. It is hoped that by calling attention to watercolor's many facets, in the light of my own experience, this book may inspire the student-reader to investigate them more fully on his own.

HOW TO USE THIS BOOK

An important part of learning is repetition, for very few students are able to grasp a new subject fully in a single attempt. In this book I have sought to avoid undue repetition, but I have placed definite stress on certain cardinal points. It is expected that the repetition will be exercised by you, the reader, through repeated reviews of parts not fully clear. Learning calls for practice as well as reading. By alternating practice and reference you should achieve satisfying results.

For the novice it is advisable to start at the beginning and proceed through progressive pages as circumstances permit. Aided by the table of contents and the running references to other themes, the more advanced student can be more selective, reading specifically those parts which he feels may be of help to him.

FREDERIC WHITAKER

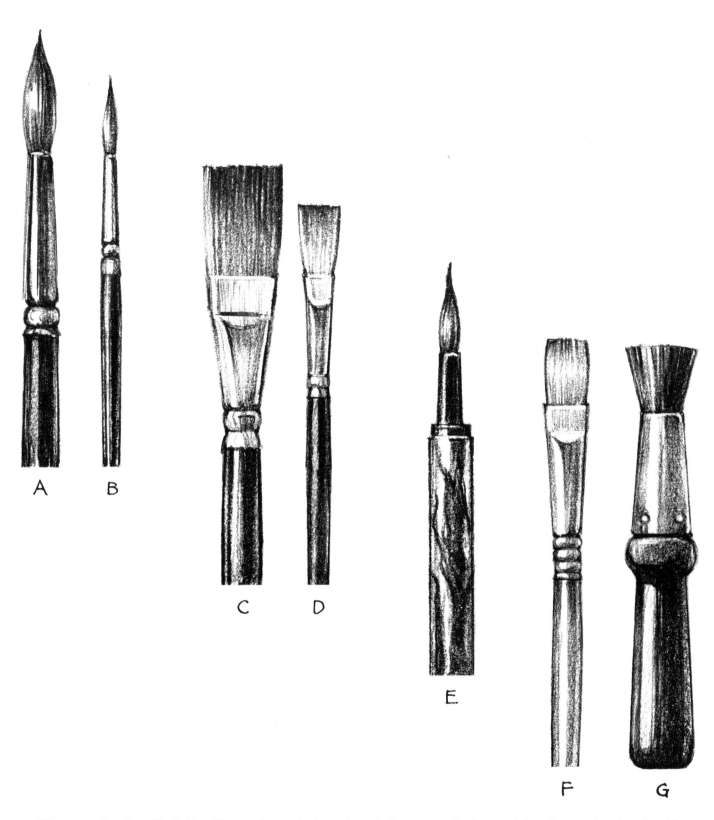

Figure 1. Brushes Used For Watercolor Painting. A and B are standard round brushes made of red sable, sabeline or ox-hair. C and D are flat brushes made of red sable, sabeline or ox-hair. E is a Japanese double-ended brush. F is an oil painter's bristle brush. G is a stiff bristle stencil brush.

1. MATERIALS AND IMPLEMENTS

Watercolor painting requires relatively little equipment. Pigments, brushes, and paper are basic, of course. In addition, you will need or want most of the following: color pans, water bowl, pencils, erasers, sponge, rag, pocket knife, razor blade, small syringe, blotter, and folding stool.

WATERCOLOR PAINTS

Watercolors come hard in small pans or moist in tubes. The hard colors are good for painting miniatures, but for regular painting only the moist tube color can be used with ease. Tubes come in two sizes: standard, ½" x 2⅛", and studio size, ¾" x 3¾". If you paint a good deal, the studio size is cheaper and more convenient.

All the well-known brands of colors are good — but "good" doesn't necessarily mean permanent. Most manufacturers make "Student Colors" and "Artists' Colors." The former are much cheaper. They are acceptable for practice work but not for serious painting. They handle well, but many of the hues are fugitive.

See Artists' Colors, page 136.

I usually paint daily, so I never throw away the paint in my pans. Twenty minutes before starting I drop water onto the hardened color so the pigment is pasty by the time I am ready. Incidentally, the dirty residue around the paints in the color wells should be cleaned out while the pigment is dry and hard. If you clean the wells while the paint is soft, you will waste quite a bit of pigment.

For my own work I like to have on hand a wide range of colors, though I may use no more than six or seven in a given painting. Actually, it is possible to mix any color or shade with no more than the three primaries, but an amplified palette can save time and effort. You simply lift from the pan the pigment nearest to that needed and bring it quickly to the mark with a touch of one other color.

See Primary and Secondary Colors, page 34.

The word "palette" describes both the assortment of pigments an artist uses and also the pan or board on which he arranges them. The following list shows my palette and the order in which the colors are arranged.

Ivory Black	Cadmium Orange	Cobalt Blue	
Sepia	Cadmium Scarlet	Windsor Blue	
Burnt Umber	Cadmium Red	Permanent Green, Pale	
Raw Umber	Alizarin Crimson	Emerald Green	
Raw Sienna	Indian Red	Oxide of Chromium	
Cadmium Yellow, Pale	Cobalt Violet	Viridian	
Cadmium Yellow, Deep	Cerulean Blue	Windsor Green	

Any other array an artist may find convenient is likely to be satisfactory. Many find it helpful to follow the order of the spectral colors as they appear in a rainbow or when passed through a prism. You can start with any color and then lay out your own pigments as nearly as possible in the spectral sequence: yellow, orange, red, violet, blue, and green. Blacks, browns, and grays can be placed at either end. Note that my palette begins with black and the browns and continues with yellows and other colors in prismatic order.

See Spectral Color and Pigment Color, page 33.

Some pigments are composed of fine particles suspended in a binding medium; others are made from dyes, or liquid color. Dyes stain the paper and are hard to remove. Only practice can tell you about the properties of your particular pigments and how they will combine and act with others. If you spend some time trying out the individual colors and mixing them with others, you will soon be able to reach instinctively for those needed for any particular purpose.

See Sedimentary and Dye Colors, page 23.

WATERCOLOR PAPER

The finest watercolor papers are made of rag pulp. The standard size is 22 x 30 inches. The standard weights are 72 lb., 140 lb., 200 lb., 300 lb., and 400 lb. The weights specified refer to the number of pounds in a ream (480 sheets).

Most of the professional grade watercolor paper used in the United States comes from France or England. The best French paper, D'Arches, has a relatively soft surface and a slight ivory color. It is easy to work with, although too-vigorous scrubbing will ruin it. Also, because of its more absorbent nature, removal of dried color can be difficult. Of the English papers, there are eight or ten different makes sold here. Half are hand-made, the others mold-made. All are good. My favorite is the A.W.S. paper which I consider the finest available. The English papers are as close to pure white as paper can be. More sizing is used than in the D'Arches paper, so the English papers have a harder surface and will withstand considerable scrubbing. There are other excellent, if less well-known, papers such as the Fabriano of Italy, and there are papers suitable for special techniques.

Watercolor board is a commercial product which consists of a sheet of very thin watercolor paper mounted on a heavy cardboard. It does not buckle in the painting process. When the paper is mounted at the factory, the surface roughness is reduced somewhat, so if you regularly use "medium surface" paper, ask for "rough" board. Though rag paper will last for centuries, a cardboard backing may begin to disintegrate in twenty-five years. If you are painting for the ages, you'd better stick to a good heavy paper, unmounted.

There is a great difference in price between professional paper and students' grade paper. Students' grade paper is made of wood pulp. A certain grade is sometimes referred to as cartridge paper. The standard sizes are about the same as those for professional paper. The customary weights for students' paper are 72 lb. and 140 lb.

Students' paper is satisfactory for practice — and for nothing else. It will not last, it will eventually turn yellow, and it cannot stand the rough handling to which professional paper can be subjected. The surface of wood-pulp paper is ruined by liberal scrubbing. I consider the "A.W.S. Students' Grade" paper to be the best in its division.

If you plan to sell your pictures, you owe it to your patrons to use only rag paper.

Watercolor papers are made with three types of surfaces: 1. Smooth, sometimes called Hot Pressed; 2. Medium, sometimes called Cold Pressed; and 3. Rough.

Smooth paper is not usually suitable for watercolor painting. It has no "tooth" so the color slides too easily down its surface.

Rough paper, in the professional grade, is difficult for most artists to handle until they have had considerable experience with it. Rough paper, in the students' grade, usually corresponds to medium surface in the professional paper.

Most of my paintings are made on medium surface paper and I suggest that students use the same until they have acquired sufficient confidence to experiment with the others. For watercolor exercises, the half sheet (15″ x 22″) or larger is preferred. Quarter sheets (11″ x 15″) may be used, but they do not allow as much freedom as the larger sizes.

BRUSHES

The types of brushes commonly used in watercolor painting are shown in Figure 1.

See page 8.

The round ones, ranging in size from the tiny No. 000 to No. 16, are usually thought of as the standard watercolor brushes. Most are made of red sable hair and are quite expensive, though they can also be procured in relatively cheap ox-hair and sabeline (dyed ox-hair). Red sable is the only available hair that will give the brush a perfect point. Flat brushes are available in widths from ⅛″ to 2″ in red sable, sabeline, or ox-hair.

I see no point in investing a great deal of money in red sable brushes, which are necessarily expensive because of the very high cost of Russian kolinsky tails from which they are made and the great care required in dressing them. Eighty per cent of my paintings are done with flat brushes of sabeline or ox-hair. Sabeline *is* ox-hair, dyed, but it seems to be of more select grade and, for my purposes, is as good as red sable, since no point is needed on the brush. My brushes range in size from ¼″ to 1½″. It is possible to apply wide strokes with them, though fine detail also can be painted, using the edges or corners of the brush. I have one round red sable brush, No. 8, which I seldom use.

My most valuable brush for small work is an inexpensive, double-ended, bamboo-handled Japanese brush. Its hair has little resilience, but it is perfect for brush-drawing, for painting hairlines, and for scumbling in small areas.

The round camel hair brushes included in many inexpensive watercolor sets are useless for serious painting.

The flat bristle brush illustrated is a standard oil painter's brush (called a "bright"), and the round, flat-ended one is an inexpensive bristle brush

See Modeling Color, page 55.

made for shipping-room stenciling. Either can be used for scrubbing out previously dried paint. The flat one is also handy for "modeling" pasty color. I also have a regular house-painter's varnish brush with round handle, somewhat like the large flat brush illustrated but considerably heavier and about 1½″ wide. This is not used often, but on occasion it is helpful for reducing the value of a color passage already dry.

The best brushes for you are, obviously, those with which you get the best results. Try different kinds until you know their possibilities, but — an admonition — don't try to paint watercolors with little brushes. Always use the largest you can manipulate for the job at hand.

PENCILS

Pencils Nos. 2B or 3B are about right. Very soft pencils, Nos. 4B to 6B, are delightful to work with, but if erasure is necessary they smudge.

COLOR PANS

Pans for holding and mixing colors are available in innumerable styles. Before definitely selecting one, look over the possibilities. If possible, see what your artist friends are using and find out whether or not they find them satisfactory.

Most artists like a large flat pan for mixing colors and washes. This may be connected with the wells which hold the colors or it may be simply one of the white porcelain-enameled butcher's trays that are now in vogue. These pans measure 10″ x 15″ or 12″ x 19″ and are about ½″ deep. Whatever your choice, the pan should be white so that colors can be accurately judged.

For making small sketches, the folding, pocket-size metal color boxes with built-in mixing wells are satisfactory, but for large paintings one needs much more capacious equipment. Today, when most large paintings are made in the studio and when outdoor subjects are reached by automobile, the compact kits of yesteryear are not so essential.

Indoors or out, I prefer to work with two standard white plastic color "slants," 4″ x 12″, each containing eight circular color wells and eight inclined depressions, 1½″ x 2¼″, for mixing. For convenience, I have had them cemented edge to edge on a plywood base. For a large pure wash I prepare my liquid pigment in a separate small glass bowl. I also like to have at hand an expanse of newspaper, which I use for testing colors and for reducing the liquid content of a brush.

SYRINGE

A small rubber or plastic ear syringe, which can be bought in any drug store, is very useful for squirting water onto the paint when you want to moisten the pigment and for cleaning out the liquid in color wells.

BLOTTER

Blotting paper comes in handy for soaking up unwanted water. Some artists use a "thirsty brush" for the same purpose, wetting the brush and squeezing out the water with the fingers.

RHODE ISLAND BARN

In this painting the sun is ahead of the artist, so all vertical surfaces are in shadow.

FOLDING STOOL

I usually carry a number of camp stools in the car trunk. When feasible, I sit on one and use another to rest my board and paper on, while a third, topped by a piece of 16″ x 24″ wallboard, makes an excellent table for colors, brushes, water, etc.

VIEWFINDER

Some artists believe a viewfinder is useful not only for finding compositions, but also because it helps them exclude distracting side elements during the actual painting.

It is easy to make a simple viewfinder for yourself. Cut a hole about 2¾″ x 3¾″ in a small piece of cardboard. These dimensions are proportionately the same as those of a standard 22″ x 30″ watercolor paper. Close one eye and hold the card before the other, moving the card backward or forward until you can see through the hole exactly as much of the scene as you want to include.

SIMPLIFIER OF VALUES

If you look through a piece of blue glass at a brightly-colored scene, you will find it reduced to virtual monochrome. Many artists find this helpful in determining values. Some combine the blue glass with the cardboard viewfinder. Personally, I feel the two operations involved are of different natures and are better handled separately.

2. BASIC TECHNIQUES

Once you have your watercolor equipment before you, the next step is to learn to handle it correctly. Watercolor is a deceptive medium — it is easy to use, but it is not easy to use well. Considerable practice is needed to learn to control it. Before you can produce finished paintings with the fresh accidental quality for which watercolor is famous, you must learn by trial and error what causes the "accidents" and how easily the freshness is lost.

PREPARING THE PAPER

It is possible to take a sheet of medium or heavy weight watercolor paper, attach it loosely to a drawing board with spring clips, and begin to paint. Many artists do just this. Others prefer to sponge or stretch their papers beforehand. Whether or not these procedures are necessary depends to some extent on the kind of paper being used. Often, however, it is a matter of personal preference on the part of the artist. Personally, I use A.W.S. 300 or 400 lb. paper without sponging or stretching.

HOW TO STRETCH PAPER

The stretching process is possible because paper expands when moist or wet and contracts as it dries. Papers of 200 lbs. or less should be stretched. Otherwise they will buckle too much when moistened. The heavier papers can be used without stretching. Some watercolorists, however, always stretch their papers, regardless of weight.

Heavy paper has an unbelievably powerful "pull" when drying, so a strong background board and a strong adhesive to fasten the paper to it are needed. A weak board will warp, and if a poor adhesive is used, the paper will pull away at the edges, with ruinous results. Let me describe the stretching of a 22" x 30" paper of 300 lb. weight, for that is about as large, heavy and strong a paper as you will ever want to stretch. Smaller and lighter papers can be dealt with similarly.

For best results use a ¾" drawing board about ¼" larger all around than the paper. Have ready four strips of heavy, 3" wide gummed paper corresponding in length to the four sides of the board. Soak the paper, mop off the surplus water, and let the paper stand until its surface is free of loose moisture. Lay it evenly on the board and, taking the gummed papers one by one, moisten them and stick them to the limp paper, covering one inch of the outer margin. Then fold the gummed paper around the edge and back of the drawing board. Be sure that the gummed tape adheres firmly everywhere. Now let the whole stand until it is perfectly dry. If all precautions have been observed, the paper will dry out as tight as a drumhead, but if the adhesive has loosened in any part, the paper will be warped and unfit for use. The only remedy is restretching.

Some artists use a drawing board considerably larger than the paper and simply apply the gummed paper flat, but this has less holding power than wrapping the tapes around the back of the board. Others wrap the water-color paper itself around the edges of the board (or of a regular canvas stretcher, leaving the center of the paper unbacked) and use thumbtacks for holders instead of tape. The thumbtacks are inserted in the back; never use them on the front of the paper or you will lose the continuous tight surface desired. The wrap-around method naturally wastes a lot of paper.

FASTENING PAPER TO BOARD

If your paper is not stretched, it must be rigidly supported by a board of some kind. Don't try to work with a loose pad or some flexible contrivance, nor on a board so small that the paper extends beyond its edges. A supporting panel of 3/16″ plywood about one inch longer and wider than your paper is ideal. This provides a ½″ marginal allowance all around. Hold the paper in place with four to eight large, strong metal spring clips. (They can be bought in stationery stores. Don't get small ones!) As the paper expands from the moisture, the clips can be loosened to take up the slack.

Some paper comes in blocks, usually twenty-four sheets held together at the edges with tape. These are satisfactory in small sizes for making sketch notes or for drybrush painting, but should not be used in larger sizes for wet work, because the fixed edges prevent expansion and the paper buckles. For the same reason, papers should not be fastened down with thumbtacks.

USING THE BRUSHES

It is advisable to experiment with your brushes and colors to learn their possibilities, as shown in Figure 2. A variety of effects can be produced by the handling of the brush itself and by the density of the color used. In-

See pages 16-17.

Figure 2. Some examples of different types of brush strokes on a medium-surface paper are shown on the following two pages. A. Strokes were done with a ¾-inch flat brush. The solid area was made with a fully charged brush held upright; the dappled area by dragging the brush on its side. B. Strokes made with a No. 12 round red sable brush. The hairline was made with the point of the brush; the heavy spots by pressing down on it. The thin lines of uneven direction were registered by dragging the point of the brush lightly, twirling it back and forth. C. Strokes made with a No. 12 round brush dragged on its side. D. Strokes made with a 1-inch flat brush charged with thick color and brushed lightly. E. Strokes made with a No. 6 round brush, lightly stroked back and forth with thick, nearly dry color. F. Strokes made with a No. 6 round brush scumbled about in various directions. By repetitive scumbling one is able to build up darks to any point desired. G. Dry brushing which was lightly stroked, with little color on the brush. H. The outer branches of the tree were painted with the side of a round brush held so that the handle of the brush was almost level with the paper.

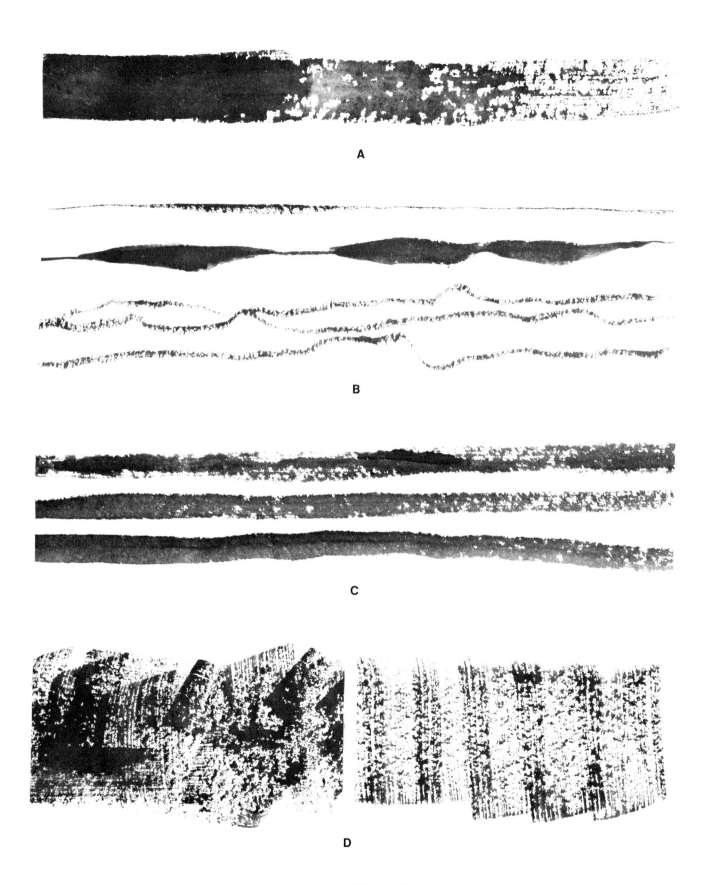

Figure 2.

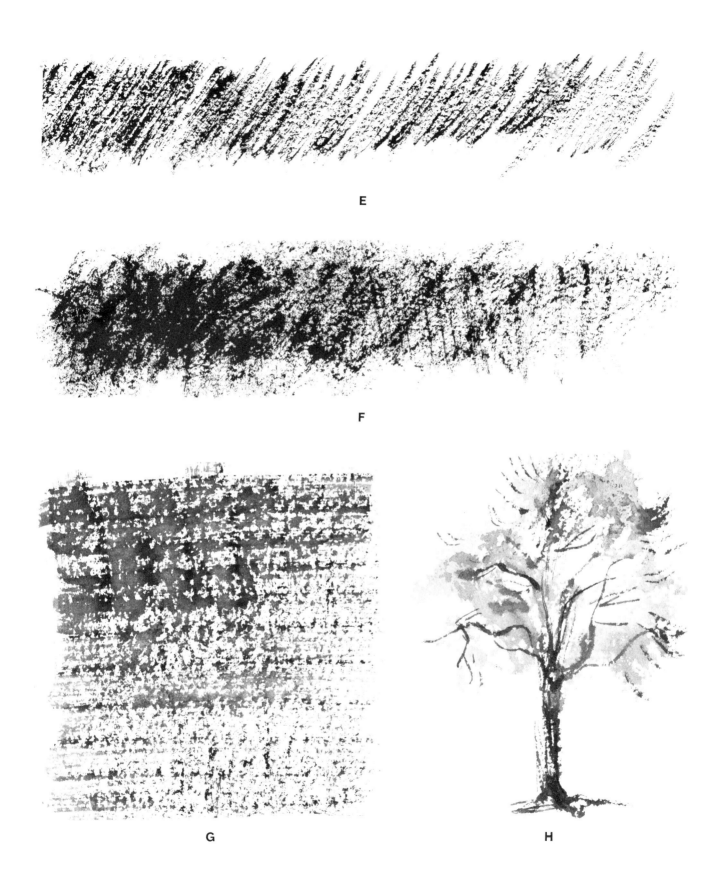

E

F

G

H

cidentally, remember that beginners invariably overestimate the thickness of color on their brushes.

Practice handling the brush in different ways. Hold it upright, swing it from right to left on its side, drag it along the paper endwise on its point. Slow brushing will deposit the color solidly, quick strokes will leave white paper showing through.

Don't be too tense about brushing. Hold the handle lightly near the end and swish it about lightly. Remember a brush is not a pencil and should not be used like one. At times you may want to hold your brush as the Orientals do—at right angles to the line of the arm and hand, with the handle pointing directly upward.

Color may vary in density from very light and thin to thick and heavy. The former is likely to leave a solid tone, the latter may register only on the tops of the paper's grain, leaving the depressions white.

HOW TO APPLY A WASH

The wash is the foundation of transparent watercolor painting. A wash is an area of color, evenly applied, without breaks or brushmarks. It may be uniform in hue and value, or it may graduate from one hue or value to another, but it should be smooth and effortless in appearance. It is used primarily to cover large areas which cannot be painted smoothly with individual brush strokes, but even in relatively small areas the wash principle applies.

Since watercolor is a fluid medium, it can best be controlled by painting on an inclined surface from the top to the bottom and taking care of the accumulation of pigment at the lower edge.

To paint a wash, first prepare a pan of color diluted with water. Place your drawing or paper on a slanted easel or board, at as high an angle as you can negotiate, and then, using as large a brush as the job will permit, begin at the top to brush the color across the whole width of the area involved. The strokes should be very wet, with as much liquid in the brush as it will hold. As soon as the first horizontal stroke has been completed, repeat the process with a second stroke under the first, allowing the collected liquid color of the first to mingle with that of the second. This horizontal brushing should be continued until the surface to be painted is covered. Now, with a brush, remove the color as it collects at the lower edge until the paper is dry. In effect, you have simply allowed a quantity of liquid transparent paint to roll down the surface of the paper, covering every pore of the area. That is the principle of the wash. There are, however, certain complications that may arise. The most common are listed below.

Is the Paper Ready?

The paper itself must be ready for the wash. It must be of such surface and have such absorptive quality that the color will "take" evenly. Some papers (very often the cheaper grades) will receive the color without preliminary treatment, but others, notably the handmade, all-rag papers, have a surface that is very dry or water-resistant. To attempt a direct wash on such papers is to invite uneven effects or white spots where the color bub-

MARKET ON A MOUND. 21" x 29"

AQUARIUM

FAR FROM THE MADDING CROWD

bles or refuses to take hold. **Papers of this type should be sponged thoroughly with clear water and allowed to dry before the color wash is applied.** Sponging removes some of the glue sizing and leaves the paper properly absorptive.

Have Enough Color Mixed

It is essential that there be plenty of mixed color in your pans, for if you run out of color before the wash is completed, it is impossible to continue the operation as planned. As each brushful of color is taken up, the mixture should be stirred, for virtually all colors have a tendency to settle. Certain colors, because of difference in the specific gravity of the pigments, will not remain mixed in the pan, but will tend to separate, thus making their combined use, in washes, virtually impossible. Only personal experimentation will tell you about such pigment characteristics.

The Correct Angle

If the slant of the paper is too steep, the liquid wash may break out of control and rush down the paper in rivulets; if the angle is too low, the color will not run freely. It will hesitate in certain areas which will dry darker than the others. You will have to experiment with this angle-of-the-paper problem, for the angle needs to be higher for thick color and lower for thin. Whatever the angle of the picture, if the paper is thin, or un-stretched, the water-expansion may make it wavy so that depressions will form in which the color will collect and dry unevenly. The color must be allowed to run uninterruptedly down the paper to assure a constant density.

Compatible Mixtures

Because of the size of their pigment particles or the character of their suspension in the paint medium, some colors can be handled in washes better than others. You will soon learn which are best for your method. Alizarin Crimson or Cobalt Blue, for instance, are easily handled in a wash. Cerulean Blue and Cobalt Violet, on the other hand, are poor colors for smooth washes. Their pigment particles are large and do not remain in perfect suspension in the paint. They form deposits wherever the pool of color is permitted to stand for a moment. This can be useful at times, but not for smooth washes.

See Texture, page 126.

Surface Differences

Colors act differently on papers of different surface. If, for instance, color is applied to a very smooth surface such as bristol board, the wash will slide easily downward and a very pale color will result. A very rough paper, on the other hand, will retard the downward movement of the paint, will hold a great deal of color in the small surface depressions, and will dry out in relatively dark value. All washes, however, appear lighter when dry than when applied.

Leave It Till Dry

Never attempt to patch up a bad spot in a wash while it is still moist. Once a wash has been laid down, it should be left until it is dry. Even a single drop of clear water released into a partly dried wash will make an unsightly circle, sometimes called a "sunburst." Any other treatment of a moist wash will prove equally disastrous. Small faults in a wash can be corrected after it has dried.

Graded Washes

Washes need not be made with colors of equal density throughout. The depth of color may increase or diminish as the paint is applied, or it may change from one hue to another, but the transition in either case should be controlled by the painter and, except in unusual circumstances, the gradation should be smooth. To vary the color or density of a wash as it is applied, prepare in advance pans of diluted paint of the two or more colors needed, or pans of colors and a separate pan of clear water. Then, as the wash is brushed on the paper, the different colors, or a greater amount of water, may be added as the work proceeds.

Where the desired variation entails a change from light to dark or dark to light, it is advisable to make the change vertically. For instance, assuming you want the left side of the area dark and the right side light, turn the paper so its left side is at the top, then start with a heavy wash and thin it out with water as it descends to the bottom (actually the right side of the picture.)

These are the basic facts about washes. A little practice will show you how to deal with them.

ERASING PENCIL LINES

Normally, very little of the original pencil layout remains visible in a finished watercolor. What does show, after wet brushing, often enhances the freehand aspect of the work. However, in the white or nearly white spaces, it may be necessary to erase the lines. This can be done with little difficulty through a very thin wash of color, but a heavier wash is likely to act as a fixative. It is often a good idea, therefore, to erase the light areas during early painting stages. Be sure the paper is thoroughly dry or the surface of the paper may be damaged.

COLORS TOO LIGHT?

Beginners invariably lay on their color washes too thin. Watercolor dries lighter than it appears when wet, so allowances have to be made for this when applying color. There are, however, other reasons for weak and wishy-washy results. Many beginners, when laying a wash of pre-mixed pigment, dip their brushes in water after each color stroke or, when nearing the limit of a wash area, fill it out with water rather than color. In either case they thin the mixture and produce a weak wash. For a flat wash the brush should move only between the color pan and the paper.

If this weak-wash tendency afflicts you, a simple exercise can help to correct it. Select small swatches of colored paper or cloth and place them on your white paper. Next, mix up pigment in your pan that you think will approximate each swatch in strength and wash a sizable spot of the liquid color on the paper beside the swatch. Let the wash dry and compare it with the swatch. If the wash is too light—as it almost certainly will be—repeat the process with heavier mixes until you are satisfied. You will soon be able to gauge the correct depth of color without hesitation.

MIXING METHOD

When I wish to cover a large area with a regular wash, I mix the color beforehand in a pan. Often, however, I mix my colors right on the paper, trying out the color there and bringing it to the desired shade while still wet. For example, if I want a certain orange-brown hue, I decide, almost mechanically, that I need Sepia and Cadmium Orange. I dip my brush into both of these colors, then sink the point into my bowl of water, deep enough to absorb the required amount of water, but not so deep as to lose the two pigments on it. Then I boldly swish the paint about in the middle of the area to be colored. If I see that the mixture needs a little more red, I add a touch of Cadmium Scarlet, a trifle more water, mix the whole evenly, and brush it across the appointed space. All this takes but a second.

SEDIMENTARY AND DYE COLORS

Paint pigments are of two kinds: tinting or staining colors and sedimentary colors. Sedimentary pigments are composed of minute particles suspended in liquids or semiliquids. The dyes are simply colored liquid. The earth colors (ochres, siennas, umbers), metallic derivatives (Cobalt Blue and the iron oxides), and certain other pigments are sedimentary. Most of the others are dye colors.

See Artists' Colors—How Long Will They Last?, page 136.

In applying tinting colors, remember that they tend to penetrate the paper and are difficult to remove after drying. Some, incidentally, have much more tinting strength than others. Sedimentary colors, on the other hand, are less penetrating and can be modified more easily. Some artists use light dye-color washes as a cohesive foundation for their pictures, reserving the sedimentary colors for the later stages, knowing that prolonged manipulation of the latter will not affect the former. Sedimentary colors can also be useful in achieving certain textural effects.

See Texture, page 126.

3. STEPS IN PAINTING A WATERCOLOR

See How I Paint a Watercolor, page 29.

No two artists paint alike. It would be presumptuous, therefore, to say how a picture *should* be painted. But I can tell you how I proceed. Naturally, I adjust my method to the particular subject at hand, but I *do* follow a general routine based on specific procedures. The steps, explained in detail in the following pages, are as follows:

1. Choose a subject.
2. Plan the picture with a very small pencil sketch.
3. Pencil the composition on the full sheet.
4. Paint the whole picture simply in flat local colors.
5. Paint in the pattern of shadows or dark areas roughly.
6. Finish the big masses, one by one.
7. Add the finishing touches.

CHOOSING A SUBJECT

See Painting Subjects Are Easily Found, page 141.

For practice, any object will serve as a subject: a house, a tree, a doll, or whatever is at hand. But if one is painting a serious picture, more care in selection is needed. An artist who hopes to contribute to mankind's store of art has no right to offer a creation closely similar to one already painted. Whatever he presents should be his own conception. Students frequently find it difficult to see a picture in the myriad details confronting them. This is understandable, but the procedure is really simple. First make sure that the subject possesses some individuality. Some feature or features should be arresting: the atmospheric mood, the color combination, the architectural or structural character, the dress of people, or some other aspect. The subject should not be banal. Then, choose a scene that would make a picture as nearly complete as possible. One can, of course, build a composition around any single item, depending entirely upon his imagination for supporting material, but this calls for considerable time and effort. So if you can find a subject that requires little change, it is foolish to reject it for a less promising theme. Don't waste time needlessly. It is better to approach your subject with an open mind, ready to accept whatever is good rather than to demand scenes that fit preconceived ideas.

So, assuming the prospective picture is to be a landscape (though the rules apply to other classifications), cast about until you find something you consider striking. It may be a hamlet in a valley or a cluster of trees about a house, or it may be nothing more than a peculiar cast of light on an otherwise commonplace object. Then, having found the distinguishing factor, look about to see if there are other secondary units in the vicinity that might be combined with it satisfactorily. If not, look into your storehouse of memory for whatever additional details are required.

PLANNING THE PICTURE

The scene before you should be used only as inspiration. If a part of the scene is poor, you should not say later, "Well, that's the way it was!" You must change or eliminate any factors not helpful and add anything that may be needed.

Every work of art is a composition. A composition is not an accidental arrangement. To lay out a composition—that is, to design the pattern of a picture—start by making a small pencil sketch. This need not measure more than a few inches and may take only a few moments, though more time may be needed. The sketch should be developed sufficiently to show that your composition is satisfactory and to reveal what must be done in the final painting. This is very important. To essay the painting of a large picture without some sort of pre-calculated guide demonstrates poor planning and ensures a waste of time.

See Composition, page 56.

There are, of course, experienced artists who by just looking at a scene can mentally change or rearrange it to make a good composition, but such artists are not in the majority. A thumbnail plan is a necessity for most of us.

For your small sketch, first draw, in the middle of a paper, the part that you consider indispensable, whatever it was that first attracted you. That is to be the heart of your picture. It may be a barn, a panoramic group of objects, a doorway, or any of a number of things. Keep the sketch small in relation to the size of the paper so that when all other parts of the picture have been added white space will still surround it. This is important. Otherwise, you will find your plan running over the edge of the paper.

Having drawn, simply and quickly, the most important feature—let us say, the barn—add other components one at a time: a large tree behind the barn, a group of bushes beyond, a small building to one side, mountains in the distance, rocks in the foreground, and so on. Extract from nature those things that are good for your picture, reject those that are useless, change the size, position, value, or contour of those only partly acceptable. The sketch, meanwhile, is expanding outward in all directions from the original note, the barn.

Now decide just where the picture should be lopped off—on the sides, at the top, and at the bottom—for you have probably extended the sketch to include more ground than the composition will need. Draw vertical and horizontal lines through the pencilled sketch to mark the found boundaries. Keep the rectangle as small as possible, excluding everything you can possibly do without.

Figure 3. Cardboard Angle Pieces. Two L-shaped pieces of cardboard can be useful in determining the size, proportion, extent, and emphasis of a composition. After a sketch plan has been made for a picture, the two angle pieces can be moved about over it to form many variations on the original composition.

Figure 3 shows how cardboard angles shaped like a carpenter's square can be useful in deciding the extent of the picture. Overlapping the two pieces to form a rectangle, move them upwards, downwards and sideways on the diagram until the size and arrangement seems satisfactory. By using these angle cards, you can change the position of everything in the picture. How? Well, suppose the barn is in the center of the picture and you don't like it there. Moving the angle pieces to the left will have the effect of moving the barn to the right; moving them up will place the barn nearer the bottom of the picture; moving them down will show how the barn would look near the top. And all these rearrangements can be tried without re-drawing anything.

Once satisfied with the arrangement, draw a pencil line to mark the inner boundaries of the angle pieces. Your composition plan is finished. If you wish, you can roughly color the sketch. Sometimes this can be very helpful. A good small diagram is the key to a successful painting.

This planning step may sound complicated but, in practice, it need not take more than a few minutes.

PENCILLING THE COMPOSITION ON THE FULL SHEET

Having carefully laid out a small sketch plan, you now reproduce that pattern on a large sheet of paper. Draw only enough to show the placement of the principal masses and picture components—no details—for the pencil lines will likely get lost in the painting process and the detail drawing, if any is required, can be done later with the brush. But accurate placement is important. Many students make large drawings whose proportions bear little relation to those on their painstakingly prepared picture-plan sketches. Of what use is a plan if it isn't followed? If the horizon line is one-third the way up the picture in the small sketch, you don't want it half-way or quarter-way up in the big picture. You want it one-third the way up—exactly.

See How to Enlarge a Picture, page 80.

LAYING IN THE LOCAL COLORS

Using simple flat washes, paint loosely the various picture areas in their general colors, being careful to keep them lighter than you want them so they can be developed later on. The whole picture, with the possible exception of the sky, should receive color. The colors need only be approximate, for they can be changed easily. The painting should be done in a broad manner—no niggling. If a small red spot belongs in the yellow hillside, slosh the weak yellow paint right over it. Remember, you are simply laying in the general color pattern.

LAYING IN THE SHADOW PATTERN

Most landscape pictures are made up of a pattern of sunlight and shadows or of lights and darks. The local color already applied represents, roughly, the lights. To add the darks, prepare a pan of "shadow color" (usually a warm gray mixture of brown and blue) and apply it flatly and loosely to the appropriate areas, using the same gray throughout, but add-

See Neutralized Color, page 99.

ing a bit of local color wherever it is needed. This finished, you will be able to see and evaluate the entire composition and make plans for its completion.

DEVELOPING THE VARIOUS MASSES

Most compositions can be divided into definite units. A group of six trees standing alone might be one; a broad hillside another. Take any one unit, preferably the most important, and proceed to finish it. Consulting the scene before you, the range of colored masses already on the paper, and your mental conception, you must decide how strong to make the chosen area, what the exact colors should be, and how dark the values. The lightly applied color already on the paper can be loosened with water and manipulated without difficulty. Now repaint the darker colors somewhat more carefully, but not fussily. While the whole area is slightly moist, "model" or manipulate the whole mass into shape. This means putting the lights and darks and the colors into proper relation to each other and inserting the amount of detail decided upon.

See Tricks in Watercolor Painting, page 43.

I can think of no better verb than "model" for this stage of the work. As the sculptor is able to model his plastic clay, changing it about until he is fully satisfied, the painter can model with pigment. Keeping it slightly moist, you can manipulate the color for an indefinite period, mopping out with a brush, cloth, tissue, or sponge, or even adding more color. You can push the color about with your thumb, scoop or scrape it out with a knife or razor blade, or modify it in any of a dozen ways.

See Luminous Shadows, page 128.

I have already mentioned applying a uniform "shadow color" to all dark areas of the picture, regardless of their local colors. Naturally, some shadows or parts of shadows must be darker than others. Now is the time to change their intensity. If you have a yellow house, for instance, which was originally painted an over-all yellow, with a strong warm gray later applied to the parts in shadow, you can now model or manipulate that shadow to bring it to the exact strength desired, introducing a bit of the original yellow into the shadow color while it is still wet. In the work of beginners the shaded and lighted sides of a single object often are so different in color that they appear unrelated. The addition of a drop of local color to the gray shadow makes it a reasonable counterpart of the sunlit side. White surfaces in shadow should receive the same initial gray, but some of the gray should be mopped out with a brush or cloth while still wet.

See Paint the Sky First or Last?, page 125.

See Pulling a Picture Together, page 128.

When the first area has been developed, go on to the others until the whole picture is virtually finished. If the sky was at first omitted, paint it now. The process described here helps to pull together the whole shadow pattern of the picture, thus avoiding "jumpiness," a common compositional fault.

After the various areas have been developed, you may still find a few parts out of line with the whole. The values of certain sections may require lightening or darkening, a color may need accenting or subduing, or a few light or dark accents may be needed here and there. When the corrections have been made, the picture is complete.

HOW I PAINT A WATERCOLOR *(See pages 30-31.)*

The Preliminary Sketch

The preparatory sketch is the plan for the finished picture. Sometimes a pencil sketch is enough, but in this case I made the sketch in watercolor, changing it by overpainting with opaque color until I was satisfied with the composition. The opaque white outline was drawn to indicate how much of the sketch would be included in the actual painting. With this sketch as a guide, I knew exactly what I wanted to do in painting my large picture.

Enlarging the Composition and Painting in the Local Color

The composition was enlarged from the original sketch. It was pencilled in very roughly with just enough line to show the positions of the masses, but with no details whatever.

Next, the local color was applied very loosely with almost flat washes. No attempt was made to follow the pencil lines closely or to set down exact colors and values. The important point was to cover the paper with color and to register the big masses in approximately correct intensities, knowing that the color could later be modeled, changed about, lightened, darkened, brightened, neutralized, or even removed. My aim up to this point was to set down quickly on the paper a representation of the *whole* picture, for a picture must be a unit, not simply likenesses of a number of different things.

Laying in the Shadow Pattern and Developing Individual Areas

The shadow pattern was indicated roughly and simply, using a 1¼″ flat sabeline brush, which was used for most of the painting. All of the areas of the picture were then developed individually—first the monument, then the right-hand evergreen, finally the house. With this done, the picture was finished except for a few last-minute corrections.

Finishing the Picture

In the final stage the trees were painted almost completely in pasty color that was pushed about with the thumb. The evergreen tree trunks and branches were scratched in the wet paint with a jackknife.

Preliminary rough sketch.

Enlarged pencil drawing with local color added.

Shadow patterns added and individual areas developed.

Finished Painting. 16¾" x 20¾"

HARLEM SUNSHINE

REAR ENTRANCE

4. COLOR FUNDAMENTALS

The unique characteristic of painting—the attribute that distinguishes it from all other forms of art expression—is color.

The beginning painter should understand color fundamentals so that when he applies his paints to paper or canvas, reason and knowledge will guide his movements, quickly telling him things that trial and error might take longer to teach. Surprisingly, many students, and even some successful painters, know very little about the laws of color although the general principles are easily memorized. In fact, it was not until Isaac Newton's experiments, less than three hundred years ago, that the world at large began to understand the nature of color.

SPECTRAL COLOR AND PIGMENT COLOR

Color is simply light, broken up into its component parts. When a ray of sunlight is transmitted through a glass prism and projected onto a white wall, it appears not as clear light, but in rainbow hues of red, orange, yellow, green, blue and violet. Observing this, Newton reasoned that light is not a simple element but the combination of colors we now call the spectrum. He saw then that a rainbow is simply sunlight separated into its basic parts by refraction through rain or mist.

To demonstrate that light, or white, is a combination of all other colors, divide a cardboard disc into six equal sectors and paint each of the six divisions with one of the spectrum colors noted above. If the disc is spun rapidly, no color will be seen at all. The effect produced approximates white. I say "approximates" because the actual effect will be a light gray. Pigment color, with which we paint, tends to absorb some of the light by which it is seen; thus, in a visual mixture using pigments, it is impossible to obtain pure white. If the spectrum colors are combined by projecting colored lights on a screen, however, pure white light will result.

White, then, is not a color but a combination of all colors. Nor is black a color. Black is the absence of color. Were there no sun in the sky, everything would be black, as it is when you shut yourself in a lightproof closet.

THE THREE DIMENSIONS OF COLOR

Color is said to have three dimensions: hue, value, and chroma, which is also called saturation or intensity. If the degrees of these qualities could be stated accurately, it would be possible to duplicate any tone of any color without seeing the original, just as it is possible to duplicate any geometrical form from written measurements or any musical note or chord from a printed score. Color meters and color systems have been devised which are scientifically valuable, but the practicing artist must still depend upon his eye for color analysis.

Hue

Hue refers to a particular color, such as red, blue, or green. It is the name by which we distinguish a color. Hues may vary in value and intensity. Light red and dark red, for instance, are both red and are therefore of the same hue. Crimson and brick red are both red and are therefore of the same hue. Color Wheel I on page 41 shows the six basic pigment hues. Color Wheel II shows a wide range of intermediate hues.

Value

Value refers to depth of color, that is, its degree of lightness or darkness. It has no bearing on hue. Thus a light and a dark blue are of the same hue but they differ in value, whereas a medium red and a medium green differ in hue but may be identical in value. The Color Chart on page 41 shows different values of the same color. The rectangle at the top center of the color panel shows a pure red. In the rectangles to its left, the colors progressively become lighter in value, while those on the right become darker.

Chroma, Saturation, or Intensity

These terms, which are used interchangeably, refer to the purity or strength of a color. Thus pure Cadmium Red is a bright red of very high chroma, brick red has a less intense chroma, and a grayed red, one that might appear almost brown, is a red of very low chroma or saturation. The word "grayness" is sometimes used as a negative way of measuring this quality. Chroma, saturation, or intensity stresses the purity or brilliance of a color, while grayness emphasizes the departure from brilliance. The top line of the Color Chart on page 41 shows seven values of a single hue. As the colors descend on the chart their chroma is reduced. In other words, they become grayer without changing in value.

For the purpose of simplification, we have shown only 24 hues on Color Wheel II and only six values and two degrees of grayness in the chart of values and chroma. Actually, there can be an unlimited amount of gradations in each department. The steps between red and orange, for example, could be measured in hundreds of degrees. Each hue can become progressively lighter until it reaches white or darker until it reaches black, or it may gradually lose its chroma until it becomes a pure neutral gray.

PRIMARY AND SECONDARY COLORS

Color Wheel I on page 41 shows the painter's basic colors: three pigment primaries (red, yellow, and blue) and their three secondaries (orange, green, and violet). Red, yellow, and blue are called primaries because they cannot be reduced to subdivisions. They cannot be produced by mixing other colors. Orange, green, and violet are called secondaries because each is a mixture of two primaries. Orange is red and yellow combined; green is a mixture of yellow and blue; violet is a combination of red and blue. Tertiary colors, which are mixtures of all three primary colors, are really grays with a tendency toward one or another of the prismatic colors. Mixtures of any secondary with either of its component primaries produces an intermediate hue such as red-orange or yellow-orange, blue-green or yellow-green, blue-violet or red-violet.

The above facts apply to pigment color mixture. Physicists, psychologists, and others interested in color designate other hues as primary and secondary. In the mixtures of colored light, for instance, certain tones of red, blue, and green are primaries. Anyone deeply interested in color will want to investigate the subject more thoroughly. For the average painter, however, it is enough to know that when dealing with artists' pigments, red, yellow and blue are the basic colors.

COMPLEMENTARY COLORS

Every color wheel, whether it contains only six hues or is made up of many more, is based on the three primary colors—red, yellow and blue. Between each pair of primary colors is the secondary color which is the product of the two primaries. Orange, for example, the product of yellow and red, is placed between them. Any two colors opposite each other—red and green, yellow and violet, blue and orange—are complementary colors. When the two are added together, the result is a combination of all three primary colors. Green, for instance, is a mixture of blue and yellow. When it is added to its complement, red, all three primary colors are, in effect, combined. The result when two complementary colors are mixed is always the same: gray. It would, of course, be white were it not for the absorption of light by each of the pigments. Sometimes, in practice, the gray will appear quite brownish. Again, this is probably due to the nature of the pigments. Few, if any, are pure in color; most have an undertone of warmth or coolness that affects any mixture in which the pigments are included.

The color wheel is not necessarily limited to six colors. It may be subdivided by sixes into as many divisions as desired, but the hue in any given sector must be halfway between the hues of its adjacent neighbors. Whatever the number of intermediate hues, any two opposite numbers when mixed together should produce the same neutral gray. Yellow-orange and blue-violet, for example, are complementaries. They should always be located directly opposite on a color wheel and, if mixed together, will produce gray.

How do you as a watercolorist use this information about color? There are many ways, which will quickly become apparent when you begin to paint. For example, if you have used a color which is too bright for the rest of your picture—a red, for instance—you may neutralize or "gray" it by adding a small amount of complementary color, in this case, green. This subdues the red, but does not change its value (depth of color). Some artists add black to neutralize a color, but black will darken it as well as dull it.

A peculiarity of complementary colors is that they do not usually com-

See Use of Black Pigment, page 99.

bine well in close proximity. A visual vibration is sometimes set up that is painful to the eyes. For example, if bright red letters are painted on a bright green ground, many people will find it almost impossible to read. However, if the red and green colors are separated by a reasonable amount of white, the effect will not dazzle the eyes.

With practice, an artist looking at any surface can estimate accurately the various colors that go into its appearance. Viewing a barn of an unusual brown, let us say, and equipped with a knowledge of color mixture, he will say to himself, "That calls for Raw Umber with a little Emerald Green." With experience, this diagnosis and prescription will operate without conscious effort. I remember the first time I painted outdoors with an instructor. Referring to the heavy clouds I was trying to reproduce on paper, he said, "You haven't enough pink in them." My reaction, though unstated, was a flip query as to how anyone might imagine that gray rain clouds could be pinkish. Since then, of course, experience has taught me that very few hues ever rest on the dead center of any one color. Virtually all include a slight cast of something else. The trained eye can sense it as quickly and intuitively as a color meter. This faculty, which starts with calculation based on knowledge of color rules, soon becomes almost automatic.

WARM AND COOL COLORS

Colors are divided into "warm" and "cool" groups. Blue is usually considered the coldest color and other colors seem cold or cool according to the degree of blue in their makeup. Red and yellow, on the other hand, are warm colors. In combination they make orange, the complement of blue. Other colors are called warm if they tend toward red or yellow. Violet and green are intermediate colors in this sense. They can appear either warm or cool depending on whether they favor blue or orange.

ATTRACTIVE COLORS

Teachers often hear students say, "Your colors are beautiful. Mine are drab. Why?" Actually the beauty of color in a painting depends almost entirely upon the way the several colors are used together. Attractive pigments do not automatically make for beautiful color combinations in a painting. Colors that by themselves are sparkling may be hideous when used side by side, particularly if they happen to be complementary. Two or three nondescript hues, on the other hand, may unite into a lilting color pattern. Although there are traditional rules of color harmony which can be studied, it is, in the long run, only experience with your own pigments which can tell you how to put together combinations your artist's eye will tell you are pleasing.

IMAGINATIVE COLOR MIXTURES

Once you are familiar with the standard color mixtures, experimentation and practice will show you how to make innumerable others and to foresee exactly what any two or three colors on your palette will produce in combination.

Few artists deliberately mix complementary colors as a general practice,

CUERNAVACA STREET. Collection of Tore Asplund. Soule Prize. Bridgeport Art League.

for if used in equal strength the two complementary pigments neutralize each other completely. If, however, complementary colors are mixed in unequal strengths, or if the two colors are each a little off-center chromatically, unusual and desirable results may be obtained. For instance, Alizarin Crimson (a red tending toward purple) and Emerald Green (lighter than the green used on the color wheel) add up to a quiet red-purple.

Innumerable "off-center" blends are possible and they need not be complementary. Vermilion mixed with Cerulean Blue produces a lovely gray-violet. Cobalt Violet and Emerald Green combine to make an attractive muted blue. For blue skies, which can be sickening when painted with pure blue straight from the tube, I sometimes mix a wash of Cerulean Blue, Cobalt Violet and Emerald Green. Spend some time trying out other possibilities.

5. WATERCOLOR IN OPERATION

In preceding sections we have covered the basic fundamentals of water-color technique. Now we are about to consider additional methods of handling the medium, special tricks that are sometimes useful in special situations, and ways of making changes and corrections when necessary.

WET-IN-WET

Wet-in-wet painting is a method of painting on water-saturated paper with relatively thick pigment, so that the color diffuses somewhat. For a painter who is skilled in orthodox watercolor technique, it is only necessary to control the diffusion.

Before beginning a wet-in-wet painting, soak the paper in a bathtub or sponge both sides of it with water until it is limp. Lay the wet paper on a drawing board, mop off surplus water from the face of the paper with a large brush, a cloth, or a cleaning tissue, and you are ready to paint. Brush in the large areas first. As the paper loses its moisture, add the smaller ones, finishing up with the sharp accents. Even line work can be added when the surface is sufficiently dry. This was done with the painting, "Vegetable Still Life" on page 52.

The trick in this method is to apply the color at exactly the right stage of paper dampness. Naturally, the color spreads as it touches the damp paper. Only practice can tell you at what point the paper is ready for the particular effect you have in mind. It is advisable to lay on just a small amount of color to see how far it spreads before painting a whole area. Remember that the thicker the paint on your brush, the less it will spread on the paper. With very thick paint, it is possible to paint quite a sharp thin line on moist paper.

While working from damp to dry, the paper can be kept moist by lifting the edges and inserting water under it with a sponge or small syringe. Drying can also be retarded by using a nonabsorbent base, such as glass or masonite, instead of a wooden drawing board. Individual areas may be moistened with water sprayed from an atomizer.

BARN INTERIOR

LA COQUETA. Collection of Herman Lehrer.

Rough paper is best for wet-in-wet painting. The deeper surface depressions hold the pigment and give the artist greater control.

WASH-OVER-WASH

Flat washes can be laid one atop the other if each is allowed to dry thoroughly before the next one is applied. In wash-over-wash painting virtually no modeling of wet color is attempted. Though seldom seen in contemporary American watercolor work, the method has been followed by many British artists, particularly in the past.

DRYBRUSH PAINTING

In drybrush painting, the brush is charged with color, squeezed or shaken out until little moisture remains, then brushed lightly across the paper. Since there is little or no diffusion of color, the effect is crisper than in a wash, with areas of white showing through where the brush has not quite touched the paper. If one wished, it would be possible to cover large areas of the paper with drybrush strokes, but this is not usual. Complete pictures are rarely painted using drybrush technique, but it can be very effective in combination with wash. Part of a picture can be painted with wet solid washes while other sections are drybrushed. Drybrushing can also be added right over a light wash. Another approach is to use the drybrush method, then flood plain water or color over certain areas to pull them together. Too much drybrush technique alone, however, is likely to have a brittle, incoherent appearance.

Use rough paper for drybrush work, so the depressions will remain white as the minute elevations catch the color.

LINE AND BRUSH PAINTING

Some pictures lend themselves to a combination of line and color. This is especially true with architectural subjects where one wants to indicate precise detail, without losing the dash of watercolor.

There are several ways to handle this technique. Some artists begin with a complete drawing, then brush the color over it loosely. Others apply the color first, then the line; still others work in line both before and after placing the color. Usually the line drawing is made with pen and black or sepia waterproof ink. Sometimes steel pens are used, but bamboo pens are frequently employed, for with them lines can be made as heavy as one pleases.

Occasionally I draw the picture with a sharp sable brush using sepia casein because, when dry, the casein cannot be moved again with water. At other times I draw the line work with standard sepia watercolor so that when washes are later applied, the lines will be diffused and merge imperfectly with the wash.

PALETTE KNIFE PAINTING

Palette knife painting is usually regarded as an oil painting technique, but there is no reason why the watercolorist can't use it too. An example of this technique is shown in Figure 4. Apply watercolor pigment to the

See Darkening a Passage or Changing Its Hue, page 50

See Pulling a Picture Together, page 128.

See "The Little Statue" and "Church of San Juan, Chapultepec," page 53; "Church in Morelia," page 6.

See page 44.

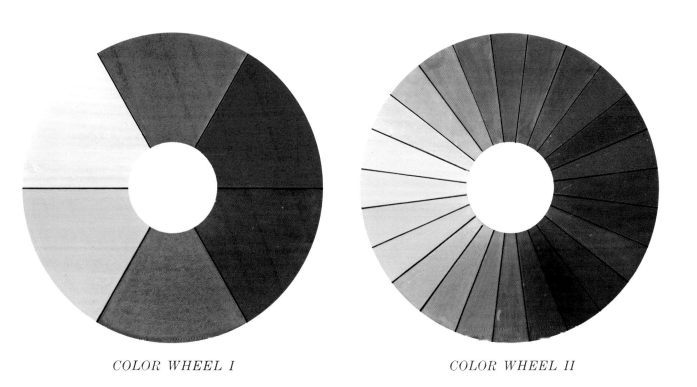

COLOR WHEEL I   COLOR WHEEL II

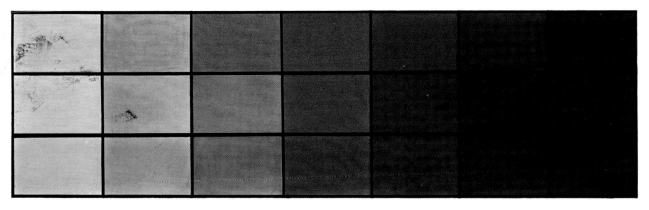

COLOR CHART

TEMPLE OF DIANA, NIMES
Courtesy Anna Hyatt Huntington, N

A STREET IN THE ALFAMA

paper. While still fluid, spread it into the pattern desired with the edge of a palette knife or painting knife. Fascinating, unorthodox effects can be obtained in this way.

STARCH PAINTING

For large, bold subjects or for abstract or semi-abstract work, try starch painting, as shown in Figure 5. Place a bowl of ordinary liquid laundry starch alongside your water bowl. Use the water for washing out your brushes and the liquid starch for mixing with your colors. Brush the color and starch onto the paper in thick applications, or cover the painting area with the starch first and then immediately paint the color into it. The pasty mixture can be pushed around at will and the color will stay exactly where it is left. By adding water, starch and color from time to time, the mixture can be kept pasty enough for manipulation as long as required. An atomizer filled with water can also be used to moisten the whole picture if necessary. Parts may even be mopped out and new color added. Manipulation is the key to this process. Any suitable instrument can be used. In addition to regular watercolor brushes, try a standard housepainter's brush, a pointed stick, a spatula, or a painting knife. Use the thumb, the fingers, or the heel of the hand for moving the color about. One artist I know uses her elbow and forearm for broad effects.

See page 45.

PAINTING WITH TURPENTINE

Turpentine and watercolor combine in an interesting way that is particularly useful for backgrounds or semi-abstract pictures. See Figure 6. With a small housepainter's brush, spread turpentine over the painting area. This will be absorbed by the paper immediately. Now, using a large brush, swish loose, watery color over the area without delay. The light, oily film of the turpentine will make the watercolor take hold in unusual patterns. If you continue brushing over the surface, the effect of the turpentine will wear off, and gradually the paint's behaviour will revert to normal. The painting can be stopped at any time. The effects can be left extremely accidental or brought under control.

See page 46.

For the painting "The Sisters Lopez" on page 134, the paper was first brushed over with turpentine as suggested above. The color in the background was left as it originally settled, but the influence of the turpentine was partly overcome in the clothing by repeated brushing. The faces and arms were brushed even more, until the turpentine effects were almost eliminated.

TRICKS IN WATERCOLOR

There are quite a number of technical "tricks" that can be helpful in solving special problems, although one must be careful to avoid placing undue reliance on them. There is no real substitute for straightforward painting. The following devices and techniques may suggest others that you can invent yourself.

Figure 4. Sketch made with thick watercolor which was scraped about with an oil painter's painting knife.

Water Additives

By adding a little glycerine, honey, or gum arabic to your painting water, you can slow the drying of the color. Alcohol, on the other hand, will make it dry faster, and some artists have been known to paint with wine to achieve fast drying. There are several commercial preparations available in art supply stores which, when added to water, enable you to paint on glass or other smooth, repellent surfaces.

Masking Preparations

Watercolor compositions often include small light areas in the midst of a large expanse of darker background color: a birch tree against a dark mountain or a white seagull flying across an azure sky, for example. The easiest way to gain such effects is to mask out the light area in advance and brush the darker wash over it. When the masking material is removed after the wash has dried, a pure white space will remain. Depending on the composition, this space can be left white or a small detail can be painted in it.

Figure 5. Painting made with color and starch manipulated with the thumb. No brushes were used at all. The tree trunk and branches were scraped out while moist with the blade of a pocket knife.

Figure 6. Painting made with turpentine and watercolor. The background shows the accidental settling of color where the paper was affected by the light film of turpentine. By scrubbing the painted area a little with brush and water, the paper surface was returned to about normal so ordinary painting procedures could be resumed.

Rubber cement can be used as a masking material if necessary, but the special masking mediums which can be bought at art supply stores under various trade names are preferable. They are more easily applied, have better covering power, and leave the paper pure white. To remove these rubberoid masking preparations, it is only necessary to rub them off with the thumb, a soft eraser, or a wad of dried rubber cement. Scotch tape and other adhesive masking tapes can be used, but the artist has to cut the material to fit the shape of the spot.

Stencils for Scrubbing Out

To clean the paint from a small spot, say the size of a dime, a stencil cut out of heavy paper or a sheet of acetate can sometimes be helpful. Using a razor blade or other sharp pointed cutting instrument, cut out a stencil of the right shape, hold it on the painting in the desired position, then with a moist rag or nearly dry sponge, scrub the paint down to the white paper. I once used this trick in painting the red polka dot skirt of "La Coqueta." I simply painted the skirt red, and when the paint was dry I mopped out the circles to a pure white using a half-inch circle from a piece of acetate as a guide. Later, I touched up certain parts with loose paint to destroy the suggestion of mechanical treatment.

See "La Coqueta," page 39.

I know one artist who always keeps at hand a piece of acetate pierced with a large number of small apertures in different shapes. Using these, he can mop out virtually any small shape.

Transparent Acetate

A sheet of transparent acetate or celluloid (the stiffest you can get) can be helpful for testing projected changes or additions in a painting. If, for instance, you decide you want to add a figure to your nearly finished picture but are not sure where to put it or how large to make it, place the acetate over the picture and paint the figure on it roughly. You can move the acetate about and change the size of the figure until the arrangement suits you. The figure can then be painted just where you want it on the paper itself.

Watercolor will adhere to the acetate if it is mixed with opaque white or if a commercial glossy-surface painting preparation is used.

Razor Blade and Pocket Knife

The corner of a razor blade can be used to scratch out white lines in dry color — such as wheat stalks, a cat's whiskers, or the like. Some artists break razor blades with pliers to make sharp cutting edges about 1/8 - or 1/16-inch wide to use for scratching out. Pocket knives are less sharp and are better for scraping out color while it is still moist. The curved end lets the artist control the width of the swath. If the color has dried, moisten it with a brush where the scrape is about to be made. In scraping out moist color, be careful not to cut the surface of the paper; just take off the color. This method is excellent for indicating light tree branches, for giving character to the bark of trees, and the like. See Figure 7. It works well with sedimentary or earth colors, poorly with penetrating dye colors.

See page 48.

Figure 7. This rough sketch shows how tree trunks and other details can be scraped out with a knife blade while the color is still moist.

Atomizer

Atomizers filled with clear water can be used to remoisten surfaces that are drying too quickly, or to soften hard edges while they are still wet. Colored water sprayed by atomizer can change the tint of any given area. When using the atomizer, be sure to keep the paper flat. Use a stencil to control the limits of the area to be sprayed.

WORKING OVER WATERCOLORS

It is often said that watercolor cannot be worked over. It must be brushed on directly and left alone. This is not true. No watercolor is finished as long as it can be improved. If an area or line offends, it should be taken out.

Some artists, particularly in Britain, base their customary techniques on repainting. They first paint the entire picture broadly and simply in approximate colors, let it dry, then mop or scrub the whole with a sponge or brush until colors merge and lighten and only a reminder of the image remains. This provides a wonderful "quality" and a base for the picture proper. Then, with deft strokes, the picture is repainted in correct colors and values. The combination of the underpainting of scrubbed color and the directly painted surface suggests spontaneity without the rawness sometimes seen in oversimplified paintings.

See Super Color, page 101.

Actually, watercolor can stand a great deal of handling. Very few simple, direct, on-the-spot renderings pass the juries of national competitive exhibitions today. Most of the prize-winning pictures are carefully composed and carefully handled. They may have been mopped out and repainted, in the preliminary study if not in the finished painting itself, for a perfect composition rarely happens by accident.

But no matter how much work has gone into the development of a painting or how much "working over" may have been called for, the final picture should appear fresh and spontaneous. There should be no evidence of the toil, sweat or anguish that accompanied its production. Since repetitious painting ordinarily results in muddiness, how can you retain freshness while repainting and correcting? The answer is by clean, direct repainting after the undesirable passages have been thoroughly cleared out. Some of the tricks or techniques that can be especially helpful are discussed in the following pages.

Removing Color

Color may be removed in a number of ways. The simplest method for a large area is to mop it with a sponge and clean water. In some cases, one can return almost to pure white paper by sponging.

A more forceful method is to brush the space with water, let it stand a moment until the color loosens, then rub the color off with a cloth. If the color does not come off easily, it can be scrubbed off with water and a stiff bristle brush. For very stubborn cases, sandpaper can be used when the surface is dry. All these methods apply only to sturdy, all-rag paper.

To remove color from a small area (up to about ½″ in diameter), wet the area, then wad up a bit of dry rag into a tight knot and, holding it firmly in the hand, place it over the spot. Press down quickly and firmly, then with a hard sidewise swipe, pick the color out cleanly. Wet watercolor can be lifted out easily with a blotter-like "thirsty brush" — any regular watercolor brush which has been dipped in water, and squeezed virtually dry with the fingers. A kneaded eraser is very good for picking out previously-dampened thin white lines.

Repainting the Cleared Areas

After color has been removed, the paper should be allowed to dry thoroughly. Naturally, adjacent colors are likely to be affected by scrubbing and mopping. In repainting, one must be careful to make repairs invisible.

Lightening the Value of Dried Color

If color needs only to be lightened a little, just wet the surface and after a moment or two press it with a blotting paper or dab it with a cleaning tissue or rag.

Another way of lightening color is to use an ordinary flat varnish brush, about 1″ wide. Wet the brush and squeeze out as much water as possible. Then, using the side of the brush, not its end, press firmly downward and draw it across the dry paint.

The strength of a color can also be substantially reduced by using an eraser on the painted area when it is dry.

It is advisable to practice all these methods on discarded paintings before trying them on new work.

Darkening a Passage or Changing Its Hue

A wash of a darker or different color can be run over a previously painted, thoroughly dry area without picking up or disturbing the under color if the new wash is brushed on quickly and lightly, without stroking twice over the same spot.

Coordinating Incompatible Colors

Sometimes adjacent colors fail to harmonize. However, hues with a common color in their makeup will usually tend to harmonize with each other, so you can simply wash any light color over both offending passages and bring them into accord. You can achieve the same effect by flooding a little of either color into the other.

See Pulling a Picture Together, page 128.

A common tint may also be useful for pulling together a color-jumpy picture. It is better to avoid an over-all wash, however, because a wash can't be set down rapidly enough to avoid disturbing the underlying pigment. One method that I have used is to blow a color mist through a fixative sprayer while the painting lies perfectly flat. This sometimes produces a speckled effect, but this can be avoided by first spraying clear water on the flat painting so the color spray can mingle with it.

Some artists prefer to tint their entire paper with a pale color (often yellow or orange) before starting to paint.

LIBRARY LION

ST. PATRICK'S CATHEDRAL.
Collection Seton Hall College, Newark, N. J.

VEGETABLE STILL LIFE. 9½″ x 12⅞″

THE LITTLE STATUE. Collection Florida Southern College, Lakeland, Florida.

CHURCH OF SAN JUAN, CHAPULTEPEC

AUTUMN IN THE AIR. 15″ x 10½″. Courtesy Grand Central Art Galleries, Inc., New York.

RUDDY VETERAN. 26¾″ x 21″

FOGGY MORNING. 21″ x 29″. Courtesy Grumbacher Collection.

Modeling Color

By "modeling" color, I mean manipulating pigment in a manner comparable to a sculptor's manipulation of clay or wax. The results can be surprising. Wet the painted area to loosen the pigment, if necessary stirring it up with a brush until it becomes pasty. In this condition the pigment can be manipulated for an indefinite time. Keep it moist and pasty until the repainting is finished. Take color out, brush new color in, move the pigment about until you are completely satisfied. Use brushes, rags, a sponge, jackknife, or what you will. The thumb is especially good for indefinitely shaped objects such as trees. Sedimentary colors are more amenable to modeling than dye colors.

See Starch Painting, page 43.

Using Crayon Over Wash

By going over a dried passage with crayon or hard pastel, you can change the color slightly, not enough to obliterate the watercolor but enough to give it a different cast. This technique can also be used for special textural effects.

Choosing Paper for Working Over

If one wishes to indulge in vigorous scrubbing, one must use a good grade of 300 or 400 lb. rag paper, preferably linen, with a tough surface. A.W.S. paper, endorsed by the American Watercolor Society, is perfect for the purpose and most of the better grade English papers will stand a good going over. Some watercolor papers, however, are of intentionally soft composition. Scrubbing will remove a "skin" from the surface which cannot easily be repaired. While soft papers have their uses and virtues, they should be used only for direct painting.

Painting Over White Casein

White casein can be used in special cases where it is necessary to paint out an area that you wish to repaint. I was once called upon to insert a motor truck, 6″ high, in the foreground of a completely finished full-sheet watercolor. I carefully pencilled the truck on tracing paper, laid it on the painting for exact position and registered the outline there. Next I covered the area of the picture in which I planned to paint the truck with white casein paint and left it overnight to dry. (When dry, casein is impervious to water.) The next day, using regular transparent watercolor, I painted the truck right over the white casein. The repair could not be detected. Occasionally, I have also used this trick successfully for correcting small areas.

6. COMPOSITION

It is often pointed out that a work of art must be a successful composition. But what is composition? Isn't any picture a composition? The answer is no. For example, a photograph is just a record of a scene unless the photographer is extraordinarily skillful artistically. A mere representation of a scene or a number of objects, whether by camera, pencil, or brush, is not a composition. A composition must be calculated. It does not come about by chance. A perfect composition is a complete, self-sufficient entity. Within its borders is found everything required and nothing that would fail to help it. The slightest addition or subtraction would sully its perfection.

A composition must hold the viewer's attention, leading his eye from point to point without his knowing that he is being led. It must have a center of interest, and one only. All other features should be secondary to the main feature. It must have "repose," which means that every element should stay in its own place and not vie with others. The focal point should not be so insistent that one's eyes become glued to it. It should be so designed that the eye instinctively, or unconsciously, sees the focal point, then meanders about through various interesting areas, eventually coming back to the focal point to start out again on another similar journey. The eye should never be allowed to leave the picture completely. A composition that holds and controls the viewer's attention this way is never accidental. As Robert Henri said: "The picture that looks as if it were done without effort may have been a perfect battleground in its making."

PICTORIAL COMPOSITION

A complete discussion of composition could fill a book. It has, in fact, filled many. For the present, however, the student need only understand certain essentials. He can return to the subject later and pursue it more fully.

Composition, one of the main attributes of a picture, is the technical arrangement of parts. Clever drawing, interesting brushwork, and attractive color can't add up to a good picture unless the composition is sound. Good composition is achieved by a tactful disposition of lines, masses, colors, values, and directions. The qualities most necessary in a good composition are harmony and coherence.

Harmony is achieved when all elements in a picture fit together in a pleasing way with no jarring discords. It is sometimes easier to recognize that something is wrong or out of key than it is to put it right. Experience alone can tell the artist how to correct it. Harmony is largely a matter of balance — balance of color, of values, of bulk, and of directions, and this balance must be visually satisfying.

Coherence means that a picture holds together. A picture may be harmonious, or well balanced, and still appear somewhat disjointed if individual parts are more satisfactory than the whole. Once the fault is recognized, however, it is not usually difficult to pull a picture together.

See Pulling a Picture Together, page 128.

COMPOSITIONAL REQUIREMENTS

In developing a composition there are several things to aim for:

1. An interesting division of space.

2. A predominant center of interest and other secondary areas of interest.

3. An entrance and an exit for the observer's eye and easy passage from interest to interest, always within the picture's borders.

4. Variety.

5. An original or personal presentation.

DIVISION OF SPACE

If you analyze many pictures, you will see that almost all compositions are based on geometrical divisions of space. The best-known formulas for picture composition are based on one or another of the following arrangements:

1. The Triangle or Pyramid.
2. Radiation or Convergence.
3. The Circle.
4. The Serpentine Line.
5. The Cross.
6. The Rectangle.
7. Enclosure.
8. Balance.

Figures 8 through 15 indicate the basic idea of each of these formulas.

See pages 58-59.

COMPOSITIONAL ELEMENTS

Other elements to consider in composing a picture are repetition, opposition, transition, subordination, and proportion.

Repetition is the reiteration of an object, motif, line, curve, shape, or

Figure 8. Triangle or Pyramid. A triangular mass, whether formed by a single object or a group of objects, is said to represent strength and solidity.

Figure 9. Radiation and Convergence. An object at the center of radiating lines cannot fail to be noticeable. However, it is better to place the center of interest (in this case the figure) somewhat off center so the attraction will not be overpowering.

Figure 10. The Circle. Anything framed in a definite shape, such as a circle, is naturally conspicuous. Again, the focus of interest should not be too near the center of the circle.

Figure 11. The Serpentine Line. Any sinuous line or direction will lead the eye through the picture. A few straight lines or directions (in this case the trees) are usually needed to stabilize the picture.

Figure 12. The Cross. An intersection always attracts the eye, but it must be carefully placed. Keep it away from the center or edges of the picture.

Figure 13. The Rectangle. A rectangle is said to suggest dignity and repose. In this case the sky is a rectangle formed by the L-shaped dark masses.

Figure 14. Enclosure. Enclosing or framing is an excellent device for directing attention. The bush in the doorway is emphasized out of all proportion to its size. The dark figure at the left was added as a counterattraction.

Figure 15. Balance. A heavy weight or mass near the center of a picture can be balanced by a small one farther away.

color to establish a rhythm or mood. Too much repetition can be monotonous, but the use of opposing factors can balance the repetition. See Figure 16.

When a line, a direction, a gradation of value, or any element that suggests motion is crossed or stopped by another factor, the point of opposition becomes a center of attention, as shown in Figure 17. The eye can follow a line indefinitely. However, if that line is crossed by another line, the eye stops at the crossing point. An area of interest, either principal or subordinate, can be constructed around it.

The eye should move about the picture from main to subordinate points of interest. The elements that lead the eye in its travels are transitional. In Figure 18, the trees form a transition between the houses. Such elements are also useful in counteracting masses that are too obtrusive. Squares, for example, are usually more striking than circles but, when overemphasized, they can become offensive. Transitional lines can be used to de-accentuate the angles.

One element in a picture can be made relatively important by minimizing others. Secondary factors can be subordinated in many ways. They can be made smaller than the major one to be emphasized; they can be placed on a lower level; they can be painted in a more neutral tone. In Figure 19, emphasis is on the central figure which stands alone. If you space five dots evenly in a line and then allow a double space and add another dot, the last will be most noticeable because each of the first five amounts to only one-fifth of the group and the last stands alone. Or if you scatter a dozen cubes and one triangle on a table, the triangle will stand out because it is unique among a large group of similar items.

Harmonious proportion is essential to the success of a painting. The focus of interest should usually be placed above or below the center of the paper and somewhat to the right or left. In landscapes, for instance, the horizon should not divide the picture in half. Either the land or the sky area should be greater than the other. Nor should the picture be divided in the middle vertically.

Size can be shown only through proportion. A tree standing alone in a picture could be any height, but if a person is placed beside it, the tree is
See page 62.
seen in its proper scale. Another example is shown in Figure 20.

Through the ages artists have made and studied rules of proportion for use in planning pictures. Probably the oldest is the geometrical formula known as the "Golden Section" which has been regarded as a universal law governing the harmony of proportions, both in art and in nature. The prescription is "To cut a line so that the shorter part is to the longer part as the longer part is to the whole." The method may be found in your geometry book, but you will be almost exactly right if you simply divide the line so that there is 38% on one side and 62% on the other, as shown
See page 62.
in Figure 21.

In practice, the rule can sometimes be used to determine the level of a horizon line or, by crossing the horizontal and vertical measurements, the point at which to establish the center of interest.

Figure 16. Repetition. Two forms of repetition: repetition of motif (the trees) and repetition of diagonal lines or directions.

Figure 17. Opposition. Without the opposition of the transverse lines, the railroad would rush the eye out of the picture.

Figure 18. Transition. The buildings might seem unrelated without the trees which tie them together as a unit.

Figure 19. Subordination. The central figure is conspicuous because the other figures are shown not as individuals but as members of a group.

Figure 20. Proportionate Size. Without the figure of the fisherman, the size of the genie could not be estimated.

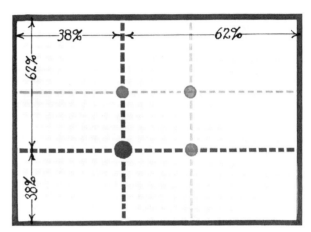

Figure 21. Proportion. According to the theory of the "Golden Section," the best place to establish the center of interest in this rectangle would be where the large dot indicates the crossing of the long and short lines of the perfect proportion. The three small dots would, by implication, serve equally well.

Figure 22. Vertical direction suggests dignity, stateliness, repose.

Figure 23. Horizontal direction suggests solitude, quietude.

Figure 24. Angular lines represent strength, power.

Figure 25. Lines bent in one direction indicate motion, force.

Figure 26. A low horizon suggests a feeling of majesty.

EMOTIONAL FACTORS

The emotional effect of a painting can be affected by compositional factors. Often the artist will intuitively choose certain arrangements to establish certain moods. In general, it is felt that a composition dominated by vertical lines will carry a suggestion of dignity and stateliness; an essentially horizontal composition may suggest quietude. Angular lines usually represent strength and power. Lines bent all in one direction indicate force and motion. A low horizon line will often suggest a feeling of majesty. Examples are shown in Figures 22 through 26.

See pages 62-63.

CENTER OF INTEREST

The feature that you wish to make the center of interest can be emphasized by color, value, shape, size, contrast, gradation of color, or by some geometric arrangement which influences the eye. Lines of direction and framing can often be used effectively.

In establishing your center of interest you must be careful to avoid making it so strong that it "hogs" the picture and prevents the observer's eye from moving freely about the composition.

ENTRANCE—EXIT

The eye enters most pictures from the bottom, where the foreground is shown. The entrance should seem inviting. Cross bars, stone walls or other impediments can act as barriers unless a way through or around them is arranged.

The exit should usually be in the distance, over the horizon, or down a road or around a corner to the land of the unknown. If the subject is the face of a building and the picture has no distance, the visual exit might be into an open door.

The path for the eye from entrance to exit should not be direct. Between the two, a number of visual passages should be constructed so the eye can be entertained on the way.

DIRECTION

See "Supper Time" and "Gliders," page 74.

The eye tends to follow a straight line, or any other directional device, wherever it may lead, so be careful that it leads where you want it to. Directional devices take many forms. A series of objects (seagulls, for instance) arranged in the semblance of a line can indicate a definite direction. A gradation of color from one hue or value to another can also provide a direction, for the eye will follow that gradation. A direction leading to the upper corner of a picture, let us say, will conduct one's interest completely outside the rectangle. It should be restrained with a transverse line or direction or some other form of stopper.

STOPPERS

"Stoppers" are compositional devices used to limit over-strong directional thrusts. Sometimes a plain sky or a simply colored foreground seems to run out of the corner of the picture, perhaps because it is the lightest area in the composition. (The strongest lights and darks should not be placed

A

B

Figure 27. In A the concentration of direction lines forces undue attention to the building at the left. In B the addition of the tree as a stopper prevents the eye from getting started toward the left and moves the center of attraction from the old house to the light side of the larger building.

A

B

Figure 28. A shows a poor arrangement. The addition of other trees in B creates an off-center mass.

A

B

Figure 29. The confusion caused by two centers of interest in A is eliminated in B by reducing one house in importance and giving variety to the trees.

A

B

Figure 30. In A the foreground and the distance are not easily distinguished. By placing the foreground in shadow, as in B, the two parts are separated.

near the edges.) This can be stopped by putting a line, stroke, or object across the eye's outward path, as shown in Figure 27. Another method would be to darken the area somewhat at the picture's border and grade it toward light near the center. The eye will seldom notice the difference, but it will stay within the picture.

See page 65.

COUNTER ATTRACTIONS

Sometimes one part of a painting is too assertive. It can be repressed by subduing the brightness of color or by reducing the value contrast. Another solution is to establish a counter attraction by using additional elements that are similar but less important. Suppose a rosebush near the center of the picture is too demanding of attention, for example. One or more less important rosebushes placed near the side will effectively reduce its prominence.

The same principle can be applied to values, masses, colors, and other compositional factors. If the eye is riveted to a bright yellow spot, a few other small yellow spots placed at some distance from the first will start the eye to roving.

COUNTER BALANCES

A tree or other object standing exactly in the middle of a picture may be disturbing because it gives equal emphasis to both sides. By adding more trees to the left or right, the trees appear as a unit, the center of which is left or right of the picture's center. This gives the design a more satisfying balance. See Figure 28.

See page 65.

DIVIDED INTEREST

Don't have two themes in your picture, two centers of interest, or two large masses of similar strength, as shown in Figure 29. An interesting foreground should be complemented by a simple background, and vice versa. The two should not compete.

Don't have important figures looking out of the picture. The observer's eye will follow the direction of the subject's gaze. It will also anticipate the direction in which a movable object, such as a horse or train, is likely to go. It is usually better to aim such objects inward. If the picture is of two persons, don't have them looking out of the picture in opposite directions.

When the observer's eye enters the picture, don't give it a forked path to follow. Group the most interesting things in the picture near each other. Make everything else subordinate. Objects isolated near the edges assume an undue importance.

VARIETY

Variety creates interest. It counteracts monotony. It can be achieved through color, form, or any of a picture's components. Variety is relative. A quiet picture, such as a fog scene, may need only a slight change in color to give it variety. This is illustrated in Figure 30. On the other hand, a picture filled with gay colors may need the addition of black and white or somberly colored area. Beware of too much variety, however. It can become confusing and annoying.

AN ORIGINAL APPROACH

See Originality, page 145.

Originality, discussed more thoroughly further on, reveals itself primarily in the artist's personal approach to his subject. It may show itself in the over-all concept of the picture, in the use of color, the design of the composition, or in some other way. A picture often tells as much about the artist as about the scene he has reproduced. It shows his way of seeing things and it may tell a great deal about the way he thinks. Don't be afraid to let your own personal reactions show even in your early work. They may be much more interesting than the successful formulas you try to copy.

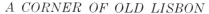

A CORNER OF OLD LISBON

7. DRAWING

Many students feel that a painter does not need a knowledge of drawing. It may be true that in nonobjective art there is little call for expert draftsmanship, although the leading exponents in that field are usually well equipped with all the academic skills, including that of drawing. In representational or figurative painting, however, some knowledge of drawing is indispensable. In fact, lack of drawing ability is the number one hindrance to painting progress. For general landscape painting a student need not be a consummate draftsman, but at least he must know the fundamentals—and the more he knows the easier he will find the building of pictures. Drawing must be learned. There is no such thing as natural ability to draw accurately, though some have such a natural interest in the subject that they grasp the principles quickly. It is mostly a matter of calculation—conscious calculation at first, instinctive later. But one must calculate.

The study of drawing demands some mental effort. It may seem boring at first to those who seek a magic formula for easy success. Drawing can be as great an art as painting. You will find it most enjoyable as soon as you achieve a little confidence.

KINDS OF DRAWING

There are two kinds of drawing: factual and esthetic. Factual drawing is the accurate delineation of an object or scene. Accurate in this case means that all visual measurements are in correct relationship to each other. It is not enough to make a reasonable likeness of the model. Even a small child can draw a simple object so that its identity is unmistakable. Factual drawing must be exact. It is largely a mechanical or mathematical process which requires only limited imagination, but it does call for a studious approach. It is not concerned with style or technique.

Esthetic drawing is the creative delineation of an object or scene. In this case the artist draws what he wants to depict rather than what he sees. He molds the facts to suit his purpose or creates a composition from his imagination.

The success of an esthetic drawing depends on the artist's imagination, taste, and skill. It is based on a sound knowledge of factual drawing. The creative artist may take great liberties with his subject matter, but before he can interpret the rules, he must be familiar with them. No artist can go far with esthetic drawing until he has so mastered factual drawing that it functions for him almost automatically, with little deliberate calculation. As Michelangelo said: "Drawing constitutes the fountainhead and substance of painting and sculpture and architecture and is the root of all sciences."

In the following pages the emphasis is on factual drawing. Esthetic drawing will evolve later, of its own accord.

THE IMPORTANCE OF PLACEMENT

The principle underlying factual drawing is very simple and embraces little more than a single factor: placement. Placement is the correct positioning of points upon the paper. When these points are connected with lines, an accurate skeleton of the scene or subject is registered. Placement depends upon two subordinate factors: measurement and direction. By direction is meant the slant or angle of lines that do, or could, connect the various points in a picture.

The rules governing placement are always the same, regardless of the scene being drawn, whether a simple prism or a Gothic cathedral. In the more complicated subjects, once the basic measurements have been registered, one simply has to divide and subdivide the areas and apply to each division the rules that were first applied to the total mass.

The novice starting to draw simply looks at his subject and begins making marks on the paper to correspond with what he thinks he sees. But what he thinks he sees is not always accurate. For instance, a foreshortened circle that is drawn as an ellipse almost invariably seems wider through its waist than a photograph would reveal it to be. Knowing the foreshortened circle measures as much one way as the other, the beginner tends to exaggerate the narrow dimension of the ellipse that represents it. In fact, he is prone to give too much length, in drawing, to anything foreshortened, whether it is a circle or other shape. Again, a cone or pyramid creates an optical illusion that leads him to exaggerate its height.

The experienced artist, on the other hand, is aware of the many illusions to which the human eye is subject when translating a three-dimensional subject to a two-dimensional paper. He doesn't trust his eye alone, but uses his knowledge and his reason and with them checks against his vision as he works. No matter how quickly a veteran artist may sketch, his mind calculates the correct position for each point, mark, or stroke before it is set down. This process may not be apparent to the bystanding observer, but it functions nevertheless.

How does the artist know the right spot at which to make his point or start a line? By calculation—by measurement and angulation. Every mark made is calculated in relation to other marks and points. The method he uses is exactly that described below, but, having been refined by long usage, it operates almost automatically, without mechanical aids.

HOW TO MEASURE

Without leaving your viewing point, you can measure the objects before you almost as accurately as if you were using a tape measure. Many artists, without reference to a ruler, can mark on paper with amazing accuracy a quarter-inch, an inch, a foot, or any other measurement. But in picture-making, instead of using feet and inches, you measure everything *proportionately:* the relation of the height of an object to its width, the size of a haystack as compared with that of the barn behind it, the width of a

LOBSTER BOAT. 13¼″ x 19¼″

CALIFORNIA COAST. 21″ x 29″. Courtesy Anna Hyatt Huntington, N.A.

ROCKY BEACH

GOLDEN GRASSLAND

FRUIT STILL LIFE. 13⅞″ x 20″. Eileen Monaghan, A.N.A.

THE BLUE DOOR. 21″ x 28¾″. Eileen Monaghan, A.N.A.

SUPPER TIME

GLIDERS

certain building in relation to the one beside it, and so forth. The experienced draftsman is continually measuring, measuring, measuring.

How is this measuring done while you remain in your painting position? As already stated, the measuring is proportional rather than actual. Drawing a house, for instance, you set down two points or lines to mark its base line and peak. You now want to know the exact width in relation to the height. To measure this you use a pencil or thin stick. Holding the stick horizontally between thumb and fingers, at arm's length and at a right angle to your line of vision, squint across it with one eye, moving the stick until its left end is in exact line with the left side of the house, as shown in Figure 31. Then move your thumb and fingers along the stick See page 76. to a point that coincides precisely with the house's right side. The exposed portion of the stick then represents the house's width. Maintaining your thumb in position, turn your hand so the stick is vertical and, still holding it at arm's length and squinting with one eye, move it to ascertain how many house widths are contained in the height. Let us say the answer is one and one half. Now, turning to your paper, where the house height is already indicated, multiply that by one and one half, using the stick and your thumbs as measuring instruments. You now know the exact pictorial width of the house. Using this system, you can measure and register on paper other subdivisions of the house and other objects in the scene. With the measurements thus accurately shown on paper, it is a simple matter to draw the various parts within their pencilled limitations.

HOW TO DETERMINE DIRECTIONS

Relative measurement, just described, is one of the two factors that insure correct placement. The other factor is direction, or angulation—the accurate reproduction on paper of the apparent angle of any line in the subject before you. Take the angle of a roof, for instance. Holding the pencil or stick between thumb and fingers, at arm's length, twist the wrist until the slant of the pencil coincides exactly with that of the roof. Now, retaining the arm's length position and without allowing the hand or pencil to twist, lower the hand until the side of the pencil rests on the paper in the right pictorial spot. Mark the angle on the paper. With a little practice you will be able to register slanted lines on the paper with astonishing accuracy.

Direction—Triangulation

If you know the length of the base of a triangle and the degree of the angles at its ends, a simple calculation will give you the exact location of the apex, or third corner. Assume, for example, that you are viewing the front of a barn fifty feet wide and that the angles from the bottom corners to the peak measure sixty degrees. You can then prove that the height of the barn is just over forty-three feet.

But without studying trigonometry, you can make valuable use of its principles. In drawing the barn, you simply mark a base line on the paper to indicate its width, then visually measure the angles mentioned with a pencil or stick, as shown in Figure 32. Next pencil their directions on the See page 76.

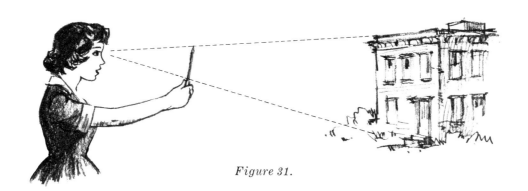

Figure 31.

Figure 32.

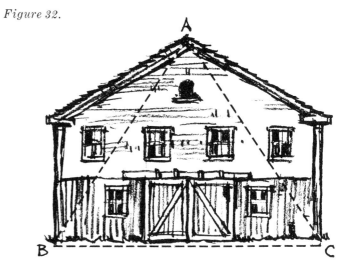

Figure 33.

paper. You can correctly register the height of the barn for your picture by placing the apex at the point where the two projected lines cross each other. See Figure 33.

Using the same method of triangulation, you can accurately find any other points on the barn—the eaves, or the windows, for instance—or you can locate the positions of other objects adjacent to the barn.

It is not necessary that there be an actual straight line in the scene when you measure such angles. Dotted lines A, B and C will never be marked on barns for your convenience, but you can easily imagine them running from point to point, and you can measure their angle or slant accordingly. This principle of angulation can and must be used in relation to anything you draw.

MEASUREMENT AND DIRECTION COMBINED

You have learned how to measure distance and also how to triangulate. In practical drawing we combine both measurement and angulation, constantly checking one against the other. When our measurements and angles agree, we have photographically correct placements. Any desired point in a picture can be located quickly if we can determine its distance from the bottom and from the side; or any point can be found by triangulation.

DRAW FROM THE OUTSIDE IN

Because of the importance of size and layout, it is advisable when drawing a likeness of anything to work from the outside to the interior. Start with your given limitations, the points or lines that indicate the top, bottom, left and right boundaries of the subject. Then proceed inward, dividing and subdividing the areas into spaces that will exactly contain the subordinate details.

In principle, the drawing of a complicated subject follows exactly the same procedure as that used for a simple object. Simply divide and subdivide accurately, and then draw the secondary parts as you did the whole. Drawing a Gothic cathedral, you would first mark the containing lines within which the major outlines would be registered. Then you would measure and indicate exactly the location of such divisions as the towers and steeple, the rose windows and the immense portals, drawing them all with simple definite lines. Then you would divide those parts into their components, and continue the reduction down to the smallest details.

That is the system to follow when you draw the specific thing before you. An idea developed on paper from the mind is drawn from the inside out, however. That would be an esthetic drawing.

See Planning the Picture, page 25.

MEASURING WITH THE EYE ALONE

While measurements and directions constitute the foundation on which accurate drawing is based, not all measurement and angulation is achieved with a measuring stick. At the start you must use a pencil or stick, for only by repeated practice with it can you fully grasp the principles involved and build up an instinctive feeling for measurement and angulation. After sufficient practice, however, most of the mechanical procedure can be dropped.

By then, accurate calculations can usually be made with the eye alone, although even the most experienced artist occasionally resorts to stick measuring to establish fundamental lines and to make exact computations.

ACTION SKETCHES

Between periods of factual drawing the student should practice making quick sketches, taking only ten minutes or five minutes or even two minutes for each sketch. This allows no time for mechanical measuring and stimulates visual and mental calculation. These sketches can be of any subject, but many artists find it especially helpful to do quick sketches of the human figure from live models.

Perhaps this discussion of semi-mechanical means of drawing will draw criticism from those who profess that easel art and mathematical systems cannot mix. However, some system of visual calculation and measurement is invaluable in drawing. Architecture, the mother of all arts, is based largely on mathematics. Illustrators avail themselves of every possible mechanical aid, and sculptors, mural painters and others who work in large scale would be helpless without them.

HOW TO DRAW A LANDSCAPE

As mentioned previously, one seldom finds a landscape subject that can be reproduced without considerable revision. But suppose you have before you a scene which is almost fully satisfactory and which you want to copy almost literally. Your problem is to decide just how much of the scene to accept and then to make that part fit the paper exactly. Using Figure 34 as an example, this is how you proceed.

After careful observation and calculation, you resolve that the expanse bounded by the dotted lines has the makings of a perfect composition. First you fix the boundaries definitely in mind. You cannot erect a visible rectangle on the scene itself, but you can erect an imaginary rectangle. Remember that the right-hand border runs vertically between two pointed trees at the right. Don't let that fact escape you at any time during the whole painting operation. You see that the left-hand border runs upward just a little to the left of the peak of that house, and you fix that fact in mind also. The top border runs through a point just below the top of the big tree, and the bottom line runs below that stone at the right of the road. If your imagination is good you can definitely see the rectangle in place. We call this "boxing the subject."

See How to Measure, page 70.

In this picture the position of the horizon line is an important factor, so, with a measuring stick, measure the vertical distance from the bottom of the rock to the top of the distant hills. Then, moving the thumb and pencil upward, you find that line is one third of the way up to the top of the picture, so you run a horizontal line across the paper one third way up from the bottom. This is your horizon line, and it is accurately placed.

Now, in similar manner, measure from the left-hand side of the imaginary rectangle to the trunk of the large tree. That distance, multiplied two and one half times, reaches to the right side of the paper or canvas. Draw a vertical line accordingly and that becomes the centerline of your tree.

Figure 34.

A

B

Figure 35.

Make similar measurements all over the scene. After filling in the details at or within the measured points, you will have accurately translated the scene to paper. Remember that in erecting imaginary borderlines you must either select an area that has approximately the same proportions as the paper you want to fill, or choose a paper of the same proportions as the landscape area.

COMMON DRAWING FAULT

See page 79.

A common mistake in drawing landscapes is that of overestimating the pictorial height of a foreground, especially if it includes a forward-moving directional element such as a road or brook. Realizing the great forward expanse of the ground, the artist feels that to show it he must run it high into the picture. Forewarned, one can be prepared to avoid such an error. See Figure 35, A and B.

The cure for this tendency has already been frequently stressed. When laying out a scene on paper, one must first set down the fundamental components accurately. In a scene of this type, the horizon line represents the most important division of the picture. If it is properly placed at the outset, the error of the over-extended road will not occur.

ERASING PENCIL LINES

When a watercolor painting has been finished over a definitely pencilled layout, very little of the pencil plan will remain visible, and what does show after wet brushing often enhances the free-hand aspect of the work.

Only in the white or nearly white spaces may it be necessary to erase the lead. This can be done through a very thin wash of color, but a heavier wash acts as a fixative so in case of doubt the erasing of the light areas should be executed during early painting stages. Be sure the paper is thoroughly dry or the surface of the paper will be damaged.

HOW TO ENLARGE A PICTURE

There are several ways to enlarge a composition from a small, carefully calculated pattern study to a full-size picture. It can, of course, be done by freehand drawing, but sometimes other means are advisable. When one has developed a perfectly balanced composition, there is no point in taking a chance on inaccurate magnification. Regardless of the method to be used, first make sure that the small sketch and the large paper have the same proportions. You cannot enlarge a square to fit an oblong without distorting the picture.

A simple method of checking the proportions of sketch and paper are shown in Figure 36. All the rectangles are proportionately the same, because the same diagonal runs through all the opposite corners. Fit your small sketch to a corner of the large paper. Then with a straightedge draw a line through the lower left and upper right corners of the sketch, extending the line until it reaches the upper right side of the large paper. The point of contact there shows the size the large paper must be to correspond with the small one. If the two papers do not correspond, either the sketch or the paper must be changed until they do. See Figure 37.

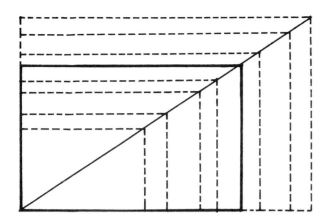

Figure 36. Enlarging a Rectangle. The heavy lines indicate the original rectangle. To enlarge or diminish it, draw a straight line diagonally through two corners. Parallel rectangles constructed anywhere on that diagonal (shown by dotted lines) will have the same proportions as the original.

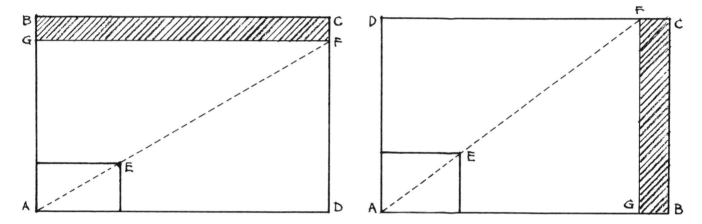

Figure 37. Enlarging a Drawing. Often it is necessary to enlarge a small sketch onto a large paper of different proportions. The rectangles A-B-C-D represent the large paper. In one corner of the large paper mark the dimensions of the small sketch (represented here by the small, lower lefthand rectangles). Project a straight line through A-E until it strikes the top or side of the large paper. From point F draw the line F-G. The rectangles A-D-F-G have the same proportions as the small rectangles. The shaded areas can be discarded.

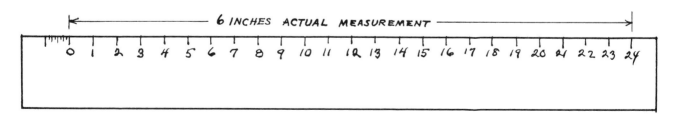

Figure 38. A handmade scale rule can be helpful in enlarging a drawing from a small sketch. If the six-inch measurement duplicates the exact length of the small sketch and the 24 divisions or "inches" represent the length of the large paper, you can make measurements on the small sketch with the paper scale and corresponding measurements on the large paper with a standard rule. Both small sketch and large paper should have the same proportions.

A common method of enlarging is to divide the large paper into squares, with lines, let us say, an inch apart. Next, divide the sketch into the same number of squares. It is then easy to reproduce the detail of each small square in each of the large corresponding squares. This is the method traditionally followed by mural painters who see only a small section of a wall at one time.

Another method, which I prefer, is the "latitude and longitude system." The artist notes certain key points in the composition sketch and then translates them to the paper in their relatively correct positions. With these key points established, it is not difficult to draw in the intervening areas. If the large paper is five times the size of the sketch, pick out a definite point on the sketch, measure its distance from the left edge, multiply the distance by five on the large paper, and make a short vertical pencil line there. Then measure the distance between the same point and the bottom edge. Again multiply it by five on the large paper, and mark with a short horizontal line. The point should lie where the two lines cross. Other key points can be established the same way. With draftsmen's dividers I can locate key points very quickly. If the sketch and the paper cannot be divided or multiplied evenly, a simple scale can be made in a few moments. With it and a foot rule, proportionate measurements can be easily effected.

See page 81.

To make a scale, take a strip of paper, say one inch wide and a little longer than the sketch is (a perfect straightedge can be achieved by folding and creasing a paper and using the folded edge). This paper is to be the scale, or scale rule, as shown in Figure 38. Lay the strip on the sketch and mark two pencil dots to show its exact length. Now measure the large paper. If it is, say, thirty inches long, divide the distance already indicated on the paper scale into thirty equal parts and number the points from 0 to 30. Each small space now represents an inch. Add another "inch" space to the left of the 0 and divide it into four or eight equal parts. These divisions represent fourths or eighths of an inch. Now use the paper scale to measure the sketch, and the regular foot rule to translate the measurements to the large paper.

Some artists, particularly commercial artists, use a balopticon or similar projector to enlarge their sketches. The sketch is projected directly onto the large paper at the exact size desired and all the lines are marked with a pencil.

ALLOWANCE FOR MATTING

See Matting and Framing Watercolors, page 153.

When watercolors are framed, about one-half inch all around the border is covered by the mat. In a half-sheet picture (15 x 22 inches), more than ten per cent of the entire painting is lost. In carefully designed composition, this can alter the pattern considerably.

To avoid this problem, you can draw a light pencil line around the four sides of your paper, one-half inch from the edge, and keep the composition within that line. Erase the line before laying the color, and then paint out to the extreme edge. When the picture is matted, the composition that you originally planned will be completely visible even though the mat covers part of the painting.

8. PERSPECTIVE

What distinguishes realistic painting and drawing from other forms of visual art is the illusion of atmosphere or distance. Perspective provides an important part of that illusion. There are three kinds of perspective—linear, atmospheric or aerial, and the perspective of detail.

In linear perspective, objects appear to diminish in size as they become more distant. In atmospheric perspective, objects become bluer or more violet as they recede, lights become darker and darks lighter until, in the far distance, all things appear to be a flat blue or violet. This, of course, is caused by the atmosphere between the observer and his subject. In the perspective of detail, details which are quite apparent in objects nearby become more and more vague in objects that recede into the distance. Perspective of detail is actually a combination of linear and atmospheric perspective, but it is sometimes helpful to think of it separately. See Figure 39.

See page 85.

Architectural renderers and engineering draftsmen require a very exact knowledge of scientific perspective, but for the creative artist a general understanding of its principles is usually enough. Often, in fact, it is desirable to violate the rules of perspective in order to achieve a particular effect for reasons of design or emphasis. For those who wish a more thorough knowledge of perspective, there are many books available. A particularly good one for the artist is *Creative Perspective* by Ernest W. Watson (Reinhold).

ESTABLISHING THE PERSPECTIVE OF A SCENE

To lay out a scene in proper perspective, we must assume that it is being viewed by an observer in a fixed position, looking in a certain direction—for any change of position will change the pattern of the lines. See Figures 40 and 41. We assume that the observer is sitting or standing upright and that his line of vision is level and does not change. The position of the observer's eye is known as the station point; the center of vision is the point at which he is looking; the line of vision is an imaginary line that runs from the station point to the center of vision. See Figure 42.

See page 85.

See page 86.

The horizon line is a horizontal line drawn across the paper on a level with the eye of the observer; it changes with the observer's changing position, as shown in Figure 40. Vanishing points are the points on the horizon at which receding parallel lines (that is, perspective lines) appear to converge. There can be more than one vanishing point, but no matter how many, all will be on the horizon line. For example, the perspective lines of a house viewed from an angle will have two different vanishing points on the horizon line—one on the left and one on the right.

See page 87.

In my own painting, I seldom lay out mathematically correct perspective lines unless a complicated architectural subject is to be depicted. For a group of houses, I simply draw the most prominent house as it appears, say about like A in Figure 43, assuring accuracy of the angles by holding the pencil at arm's length and testing it against the lines of the subject. Next, I decide where my eye level is on the house. If I find that it is one-third the height of the house, I put a mark there and draw the horizon line across the whole paper (B). Then, drawing lines through the various corners of the house, I find where the vanishing points are (C). Finally, using those vanishing points and the horizon line, I draw in other details of the house and neighboring buildings (D).

Ordinarily, this layout work is done freehand and in less time than it takes to describe the procedure, but until the beginner has had some practice along this line, it may be advisable to use a straightedge, at least for the principal lines.

Several paintings reproduced in this book represent special problems in perspective. Architectural subjects, for instance, usually require more careful perspective layouts than landscapes. In the portrait of "St. Patrick's Cathedral" on page 51, you will notice that all vertical lines slant inward and tend to merge at some point in space above the spires. This not only is in accordance with the effects of perspective commonly observed when one looks upward, it also is a compositional device to carry the eye to the steeple tops, thus stressing the structure's height.

"A Street in Alfama" on page 42 was another kind of exercise in perspective. It was only by a very calculated perspective layout that the street was made to run downhill.

PLACING FIGURES IN A PICTURE

Normally, we pay more attention to a living figure than to any of a picture's other component parts. A figure is noticeable out of all proportion to its size, shape, or color. It may appear more impressive than a building or a tree many times its size. Because of this phenomenon, we must exercise the greatest care in placing a figure in a pictorial composition or its prominence may completely upset the picture balance.

See Figures in a Scene, page 120.

When figures are secondary parts of the scene, I usually insert them as the last details in the composition. To decide on the correct position for each figure, I place a piece of transparent acetate over the picture in the general location I wish to place it. Then I paint a tentative, roughly indicated figure on the acetate. When I am certain of what I want, I paint the figure correctly on the paper.

See Transparent Acetate, page 47.

In the long run, this method saves a great deal of time. It also saves the surface of the paper and the freshness of the aquarelle, for all experimentation is done on the acetate and no actual painting is started on the paper until I know exactly what I want to do.

SIZING FIGURES

The beginner is often confused by the problem of indicating the correct pictorial size of figures in relation to each other. Placing and sizing figures

Figure 39. Linear and aerial perspective, plus perspective of detail, project the eye into the extreme distance.

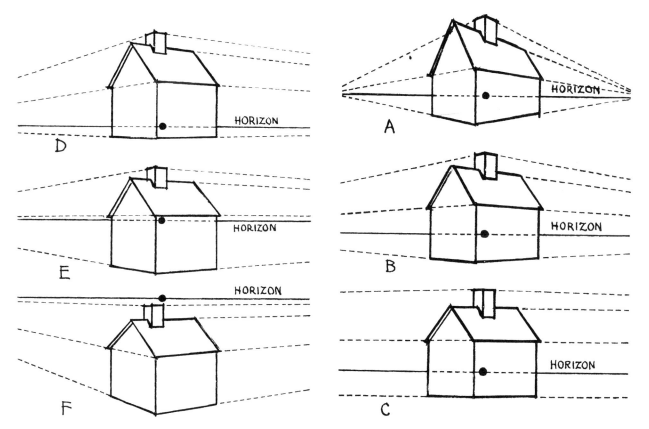

Figure 40. Height of Eye Level. Perspective changes as the center of vision is raised or lowered. D shows a house as seen when the position of observer's eye is only a few feet from the ground. In E, the eye level is about at the eaves. In F, the entire house is seen from above.

Figure 41. Distance From Subject. The acuteness of the angles of perspective changes according to·the distance of the observer from the subject. A shows a close-up view of a house. B is a more distant view of the same house. C is a telescopic-camera view of the house from a mile away.

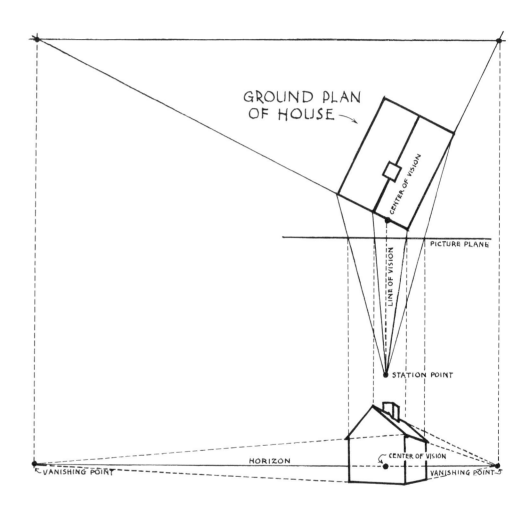

Figure 42. Perspective Drawing. To construct the perspective view shown in the bottom drawing, we begin with a ground plan of the house. We wish to draw the house on a flat plane indicated by the line CD. First, locate the station point (the position of the observer's eye) at an arbitrary distance from the plan (which represents the building). To locate the vanishing points, extend two sides of the plan to the line AB at the top. Drop two perpendiculars to the horizon line; the two points of intersection are the vanishing points. The farther away you place the line AB from the plan, the farther apart the vanishing points will be.

Next, draw lines from the station point to corners of the plan. At the points where these lines intersect the picture plane, drop perpendicular lines which establish the width of the house.

In most landscape drawings, the exact heights of buildings are not known and the artist must use his visual judgment to establish height.

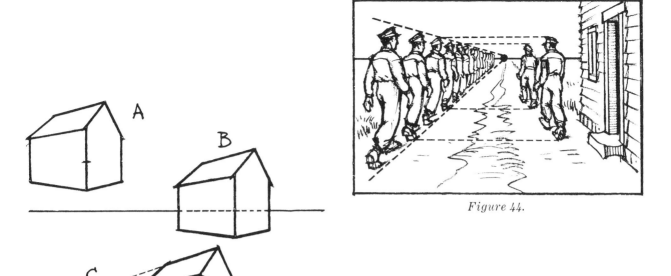

Figure 44.

Figure 43.

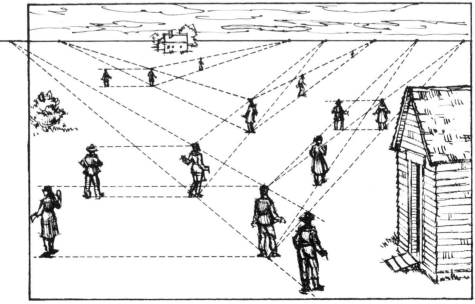

Figure 45.

is simply a matter of elementary perspective, the same linear perspective that applies to buildings and other structural masses. You can understand more easily the relative size of figures spotted throughout a picture if you visualize a file of soldiers extending into the distance and remember that lines drawn through their heads and feet will converge at a point somewhere on the horizon. See Figure 44. Drawn in this manner, each soldier will be the correct size for his position in the composition.

See page 87.

The same rule applies when figures are scattered about the picture in apparently accidental spacing. If you retain two soldiers of the file, widely separated from each other, then erase the two perspective lines and all the other soldiers, there will then remain no apparent connection between the two figures, but their relative sizes will be correct.

Again using the file of soldiers, you could move them across the paper to the right or left and their sizes would still be correct. Perspective causes the pictured size of any object to diminish as it is carried farther from the observer's eye, but all objects of the same physical size that stand on a horizontal line will all be of the same size in the picture.

See page 87.

Figure 45 shows how this principle can be applied when spotting figures in various parts of a picture. Knowing that lines drawn through the heads and feet of any straight file of figures must meet at some point on the horizon, insert the largest figure, that is, the largest in pictured size, in what you consider its correct position in the picture. You can calculate its size by comparison with nearby objects.

Now, to insert another somewhat more distant figure, make a dot with a pencil where the second figure must stand. Then, from the feet of the first figure (lower right), draw a straight line through the new dot using a straightedge and a pencil and extending it until it hits the perspective horizon. Mark another dot there. From it, extend another straight line to the top of the head of the first figure. You already have the position of the feet of the second figure. From that locating dot, draw a vertical line upwards until it reaches your second diagonal. The length of that vertical line will show the exact height for a figure standing in that position. In fact, a vertical line drawn anywhere within the two diagonals will give the correct height for that location. Repeat the process, remembering that you can run the diagonal lines from either the original figure or any of the newly established ones. The diagonal lines must always converge on the horizon line.

These calculations are based on the supposition that all figures are of the same physical height. If you wish to indicate a smaller or larger person, raise or lower the head. Do not change the position of the feet, for that would change the location of the entire figure. Adjustments must also be made in the drawing if the terrain varies from absolute level.

TO DIVIDE RECEDING DISTANCES

Occasionally you may want to draw a series of evenly spaced or similarly shaped objects along a receding line. The rules of perspective can help you to place them accurately.

Figure 46, for instance, shows how to add seven evenly spaced trees be-

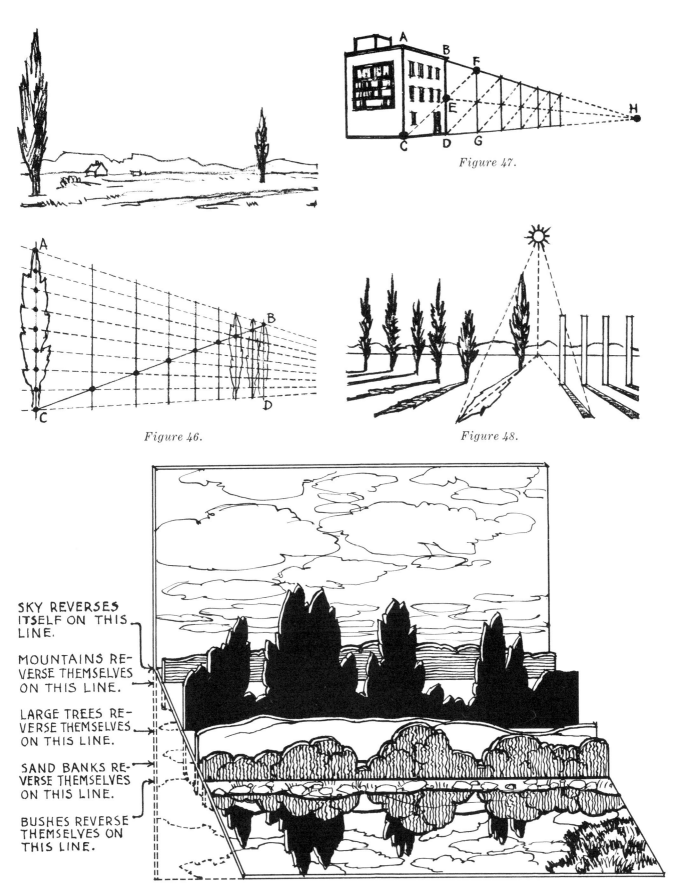

Figure 47.

Figure 46.

Figure 48.

SKY REVERSES
ITSELF ON THIS
LINE.

MOUNTAINS RE-
VERSE THEMSELVES
ON THIS LINE.

LARGE TREES RE-
VERSE THEMSELVES
ON THIS LINE.

SAND BANKS RE-
VERSE THEMSELVES
ON THIS LINE.

BUSHES REVERSE
THEMSELVES ON
THIS LINE.

Figure 49.

tween two established trees some distance apart. Draw lines through the tops and bottoms of the two trees, with the lines meeting at the appropriate vanishing point. Now divide evenly the line AC so it is marked off with nine points. From each point, draw a line to the vanishing point. Next, draw a diagonal from C to B (or from A to D). At the points where the diagonal and the vanishing points cross, draw vertical lines. Notice that the pictorial space between them gets smaller as they recede into the distance.

The same formula can be used to divide accurately any receding distance. If, for instance, your layout shows a simple building and you want to add a series of similar adjoining ones, you can determine the lateral measurements of the additional ones as shown in Figure 47. The heavy lines indicate the original building. Continue lines AB and CD to their vanishing point. Insert line EH (E is exactly halfway between B and D). Construct line CF, running it through E. At E, drop a line vertically to point G. This line shows the exact pictorial width of the next building. The process can be continued as far as desired.

See page 89.

PERSPECTIVE OF SHADOWS

The shadows cast by trees naturally follow the rules of linear perspective. The trees and posts shown in bright sunlight in Figure 48 have been simplified to demonstrate the point.

See page 89.

To lay out the shadows accurately, drop a line from the sun, which may be above the top of the painting, until it strikes the horizon line. From that point, with a straightedge, draw lines passing through the bases of the trees or posts and others from the sun across their tops. The projections will correctly indicate the shadow positions. Note that the shadows become wider as they approach the viewer.

THE RULE OF REFLECTION IN WATER

Smooth water makes a nearly perfect mirror. In a landscape picture the reflections are painted as though there were really an inverted panorama under the shores of the pond or pool. This is confusing to many artists. Knowing that a mirror reverses everything perfectly, they trace the scene already depicted on the paper, reverse the tracing, then paint the inverted details as mirror images of the upright ones. This seems quite plausible, and would be accurate were the artist's eye level exactly at the water level. Few pictures, however, are painted from that position. Ordinarily, the artist's eye level is at a point four or more feet above the ground. While it is true that each part of the scene is reflected in exact reverse, one must reckon with perspective and the eye level of the artist. The details do reverse themselves, but the landscape beyond the water does not reverse itself as a unit.

The rule for landscape reflections in water is that any object above water will reverse itself along the horizontal line of its own base at a level where that base would be if the water extended back that far.

What this rule means is that each separate silhouette observed in a receding scene—a scene containing quiet water in the foreground—has the

PORTRAIT OF EILEEN. Collection National Academy of Design, New York.

STREET IN LA ALBERCA. 21" x 29"

THE OLD TOWN, GERONA. 21" x 29"
Courtesy Parrish Art Museum, Southampton, New York.

FAMILY PICNIC

DAY IS DONE

MOORISH GATE, CARMONA. 21" x 22"

base of its own reversal at a different level in the picture. As details recede into the distance, they are indicated on the paper at progressively higher points.

When a landscape recedes, it recedes continuously, that is, there is no physical break in the actual terrain. But visually a landscape consists not of an unbroken surface, but of a series of separate outlines, or silhouettes, set one beyond the other like stage scenery. In Figure 49, for example, just beyond the farther edge of a pool there is a horizontal row of low bushes, and beyond that, running from left to right, a sandy ridge. Then there are several groups of large trees, and in the distance a line of mountains rising from the far edge of the plain. Beyond the silhouette of the mountains there are clouds in the sky.

See page 89.

Now to reflect these things accurately in the foreground pool, it is necessary to think of each of these silhouettes separately, as painted stage settings. The upright painted scene, as an entirety, will not reverse itself. But each of the silhouettes will reverse itself, separately from the others, on its own horizontal base line, and its base line is at water level. If the low bushes, for instance, are growing on ground six feet above water level, the base line is not the bottom line of the bushes, but a point six feet down in the ground.

Now, having established that base line, make a tracing, either literally or mentally, of the bushes, reverse the tracing on the line just mentioned, and paint in that part of the reflection that falls within the pool area. Then move forward again into the scene (that is, slightly upward in the picture), establish the horizontal base line of the sand banks at water level, and repeat the process of reversal. You will notice that much less of the sand bank appears in the pool reflection than shows in the upright scene, due to the constantly rising reversal lines of the receding silhouettes. Continuing upward in the picture, the tall trees will show somewhat in the water reflection, but of the distant mountains no trace will be seen in the water. They are too high in the picture. The clouds in the sky should be reversed on a line coinciding with the picture horizon (that is, a line level with the artist's eye). As for the colors of reflection, remember that they are somewhat darker than those of the scene itself.

So much for smooth water. Should the water be undulant or rippled, the reflections will be distorted accordingly. The inverted image will then consist of a series of separate, small, horizontally shaped reflections, each representing the near surface of a single undulation. These individual reflections will be separated from each other by bands of light where the crests of the undulations mirror the sky. The reflection as a whole pattern will extend downward in the picture considerably lower than the actual scene extends upward. The greater the activity of the water, the longer or deeper the reflections will show in the picture.

See "Day Is Done," page 93.

As water becomes increasingly rough, the reflections lose their definition, until nothing remains to suggest object reflections other than vague color forms. Very rough water usually corresponds to the color of the sky—blue sky, blue water, gray sky, gray water—and the water is much darker in value than the sky.

9. ADVANCED COLOR STUDY

The fascinating subject of color has many aspects, and those students who wish to pursue it more fully can find books devoted to each of its facets. The average painter, however, can best learn about color by experimenting with his own pigments. When he has mastered the basic laws regarding pigment mixture, there are still many areas to be investigated. Perhaps the two most important to a painter are the visual effects of colors when seen in combination and the physical behavior of pigments in combination. Often, in practice, the two overlap as you will quickly discover.

COLOR RELATIVITY

Everyone who is at all sensitive to color has noticed that objects often seem to change color when viewed in different lights or in close proximity to objects of another color. A chair, for instance, that appears to be an uncompromising blue in the daylight may seem gray in lamplight, blue-green against a reddish violet background and blue-violet against a green background. It's all a matter of color relativity.

To demonstrate this phenomenon, a teacher showed his student artists a picture of a child kneeling in a darkened room at the side of a bed with a multicolored patchwork quilt, then asked various students to name the different colors. After all had designated a certain square as "yellow," he covered the whole picture with a sheet of white paper pierced with a hole through which the square in question was exposed. The "yellow" was a pure green. The artist had given a strong bluish cast to the entire scene, representative of night, so that the green seemed yellow in relation to the over-all blueness.

All colors are affected by their immediate neighbors. The scientific reasons for the various changes that appear to take place are too involved for discussion here. However, the most important effect can be described briefly: When two colors are placed in close proximity, each one appears to subtract its own color from its neighbor or, reversely, to add its own complement to the other. For example, red next to orange tends to subtract the red from the orange, making it appear yellower. Purple next to blue tends to add its complement (yellow) to the blue, making it appear greener. In the case of the patchwork quilt, the over-all blue tone extracted the blue from the green and made the green seem yellow.

The rule of relativity may seem difficult to remember, but if you memorize the following list, it will serve you well.

Red makes adjacent colors look greener.

Orange makes adjacent colors look bluer.

Yellow makes adjacent colors more violet.

Green makes adjacent colors appear redder.

Blue makes adjacent colors seem more orange.

Violet makes adjacent colors look yellower.

Relativity applies not only to hue against hue, but also to dark colors versus light colors, dull colors versus bright colors, large masses versus small masses, and, in fact, to all combinations of opposites.

Dark colors emphasize the lightness of contiguous colors, and vice versa. As one painter puts it, "It is the shadow that makes the sun shine." You will have a difficult time representing bright sunlight without shadows.

Dull or dirty colors make adjacent colors seem brighter, while the bright ones tend to make the dull ones even duller. Take a drab-looking area such as a stone wall in solid dirty gray shadow, add a few definite accents of even darker gray, and immediately the shadow will appear transparent and lively.

Using only subdued colors, one can sometimes develop a sparkling low-key composition by judiciously playing one against the other. For discipline, some artists occasionally restrict themselves to a neutralized palette using Raw Sienna or Raw Umber for yellow, Indigo or Payne's Gray for blue, and Indian Red for red.

COLOR COMBINATIONS

A musical chord can be infinitely more pleasing than a single note, but its success depends upon the relation of the notes within the chord. The same is true of color chords. To work out a color pattern for a picture, start with one dominant color. Then, referring to the scene or subject or to your imagination, decide what other color or colors will harmonize with the first. Even when painting directly from nature, it is necessary to weigh the suitability of the color of each part, accepting only those that harmonize with the dominant color. If a color does not agree, it should be changed.

There is no arbitrary limit to the number of colors that may be used. You may use four, five or more colors in your composition if you wish, but remember that none of the subordinate hues should equal in importance the dominant one.

The importance of color in a picture depends on two factors: the size of the color area and the brilliance of the hue chosen. Thus, a small bright red space is likely to be more noticeable than a much larger gray-brown one. Be sparing with the gaudy colors. A good formula is to have large areas of muted colors, grays, browns, and olives, contrasted with much smaller areas of intense color.

Art supply stores sell packages of 3″ x 5″ colored papers which include hundreds of different hues, shades, and tints, collated in spectrum order.

Some artists make their own color samples on similar cards. Either can be very useful for suggesting color chords. With a white or black paper on the table, drop upon it swatches of the approximate colors and relative sizes you would like to use and see if they harmonize well. If necessary, substitute other tints or shades until the combination is complete. Then follow the general formula in the actual painting.

THE IMPORTANCE OF VALUE

Any color can have a great many values and the value is infinitely more important than color. As mentioned earlier, the value of a color is its depth of color. Pale blue is light in value, and dark blue is dark in value. A medium blue and a medium red are entirely different in appearance though they may be exactly the same in value. For many it is difficult to separate value from color and to determine whether the values of a variety of colors are the same or different.

It is useless to say that a given tree, for instance, is green without defining its value. Green may be nearly white or nearly black, or any tint or shade in between.

Different colors of equal value have a tendency to merge visually. Changing the value of one will tend to separate them. For example, to suggest distance between a nearby tree and a distant mountain, the two must differ in value.

It is not necessary for the hue of every object in a painting to exactly match its hue in nature, but it is essential that values correspond to each other properly. A great range of value can completely upset the picture's visual balance. A tree, to take a single example, may show a great deal of detail and strong contrast between its lighted and shaded spots, but it will also have an over-all value that may be quite different from neighboring parts of the picture. It is this over-all value that holds the tree together artistically. In painting the tree, the student may render the light parts lighter than the sky and the dark parts so dark that the tree is no longer a cohesive unit. This should not be done. The tree as a whole must be lighter or darker than the over-all values of the adjacent parts of the picture from which it is to be separated. The rule applies to every part of your picture pattern.

ASSESSING THE COLOR OF A SUBJECT

Many beginners wonder if they will ever learn to assess the exact local colors of a subject and be able to duplicate them with the pigments on their palettes. Such ability comes only as a result of long practice, a knowledge of the rules and theories of color, an analytical eye, and thorough familiarity with the characteristics of the pigments in one's color pan. But while you are gaining such knowledge and experience, keep in mind that the relation of the colors in the picture to each other is far more important than their relation to the colors in the scene. In your painting, you may often have to change individual colors to make them harmonize with each other. Whether or not they match the subject is irrelevant. The painter is an artist, not a camera.

Eventually, of course, you will develop a more sensitive and analytical eye. You will learn to see the subtle differences and to detect the chroma content of each muted color passage. You should also, of course, acquire complete familiarity with the actual pigments in your palette. Then, after practice, you will be able to scan any given color and know instinctively that it will require, say, Sepia with a touch of Cadmium Orange, or Cadmium Red and Cadmium Yellow, with a bit of Cobalt Blue to gray the mixture slightly.

NEUTRALIZED COLOR

Most painting is actually done with tertiary, or neutralized, colors. It is seldom that a color is used at full saturation. Many of the colors used might be called grays, that is, gray with a yellow tinge, or gray inclined toward red or blue.

Tertiary colors can be mixed from any number of pigment combinations. Thus, the grayed color produced by the red, yellow and blue combinations mentioned above could be duplicated in a mixture of Raw Umber and Cadmium Orange. In fact, you could start with any color in your pan and then add one or more additional pigments to create the particular grayed tint or shade you have in mind.

For my own work, I usually keep on hand, in one or more mixing pan wells, a residue of earlier mixings which I call "dirt colors" or "shadow colors"—both warm grays and cool grays. When I need a grayed hue, I start with the dirt color and add whatever is needed of red, yellow and blue.

USE OF BLACK PIGMENT

The careless use of black can have unfortunate consequences, making grays and shadows appear funereal. If used judiciously, however, black is a useful color.

Don't use plain black or watered black for shadows. A more luminous gray results from mixing browns with blues, browns with greens, or complementary colors with each other. Cobalt Blue and Raw Umber make a good gray which can be made cooler with more blue or warmer with more brown.

When I use black I seldom leave it pure unless the subject is black, such as a black velvet dress. For a very dark accent I might first apply a blob of black, then while that is still wet, add a drop of local color and leave it to mingle unevenly with the black. This gives a bit of life to the dark and counteracts the funereal appearance.

One of the Old Masters admonished: "Never paint any passage so dark that it couldn't be made even darker." It is generally agreed that darks can be made more intense than pure black by mixing two or three dark, pure colors such as Thalo Blue, Thalo Green and Alizarin Crimson. Of course no such mixture can really be darker than black, but its vibrancy will make it appear so.

I use Sepia more often than black for extreme darks. Applied at full saturation it is almost as dark as black, but has more life and warmth. If necessary, I add blue, green, or red to the Sepia.

CHINESE WHITE WITH WATERCOLOR

Despite a traditional feeling to the contrary, there is no reason why Chinese White or other opaque whites cannot be used in connection with transparent watercolor, provided the picture is planned that way and the treatment acknowledges the method. Many artists use opaque color to pick out light spots on an otherwise finished painting. Chinese White does not have the lucency of clear white paper, however, and its use to overcome errors in a picture patently intended as a transparent rendering is usually not at all satisfactory.

VIVID GREENS

My own palette includes five greens. By adding a touch of other colors to these five, I can quickly produce a wide range of verdant hues: light, dark, grayed, yellowed or bluish, thus avoiding monotony in my green passages. Alizarin Crimson mixed with Viridian can provide a really new note: a green violet. Oxide of Chromium seems a very dull green in the pan, but can be excellent for reproducing bright grass.

Greens in nature are usually a good deal darker, as well as less brilliant, than we think. If you hold a spectrum-green card at arm's length against a background of natural green, you can see that the latter looks dull by comparison. Then check a sunlit tree or a lawn against a blue sky, and you will note that even the sunlit parts are considerably darker than the sky. Yet many students use too pure or too pale a green wash in the mistaken conviction that sunlit verdure is bright or close to white. It is good practice to start your trees and grass with a fairly substantial green, use that for your lighted areas, and then darken the shadows relatively.

Green is such an all-pervading color that at times it becomes monotonous in a picture unless care is taken to subdue it somewhat or to introduce variety of shade and value. For a long period, prior to about 1900, traditional artists were so alert to the possible danger of green in a picture that its use was virtually taboo. Trees were painted in brown. That is an extreme measure, but it is advisable in painting an all-green landscape to exaggerate the natural differences of shade, value, and grayness. Some of the trees, or groups of trees, can be rendered a little more yellow, a little more blue, darker, lighter, or grayer. Watch the greens carefully as you apply them. It is better to understate than overstate. A symphony of greens can be magnificent but a monotony of green is unbearable. Too vivid passages can be reduced by washing a film of violet or red over them.

AUTUMN COLORS

Fall maples and oaks in New England provide a blaze of reds, yellows, and greens probably unsurpassed in the world, and many artists translate this color to paper or canvas in screaming hues. But few people can stand prolonged excitement. The splendor of the autumn foliage is enchanting because of its contrast with the staid colors of the other seasons. Actually, autumn colors are not as glaring as we think. Comparisons made with color swatches or with color meters show that the arboreal colors are far from pure. Nor does nature provide a whole forest of red or yellow. It includes a good deal of gray, green, and brown. The artist, however, is likely to extract only brilliant individual features and paint them in even more vivid pigments direct from the tube. This is a case where understatement is more eloquent than hyperbole. Shouting is not required.

The actual model for the painting "Ruddy Veteran" on page 54 was unbelievably red, but to make it acceptable for long-time viewing all areas were grayed somewhat. Inspection will show that washes of complementary green have been flooded over the whole tree, especially at the top. The finished tree is still sufficiently brilliant, especially in relation to its neighboring muted colors.

See "Autumn in the Air," page 54.

SUPER COLOR

Every painting has an over-all super color that is more important than the hue of any of the individual parts — a yellowish flush, a pinkish cast, a blue-gray appearance. At an exhibition of paintings by different artists a glance will show how the over-all color (or color combination) of one painting differs from that of its neighbor. The super color is usually the prime indicator of the mood of the picture. A fog scene is often an over-all gray; a tragic scene may be blue-black; and Arizona sunshine is likely to be a warm orange-brown.

Eileen Monaghan, two of whose paintings are shown on page 73, has painted a number of Spanish wheat fields with a fascinating golden glow. To achieve the foundation for this effect, she flooded a very pale wash of Cadmium Orange over the whole paper before painting. This gave a suggestion of gold to every part of the finished work. In painting the picture she of course developed further the golden grain areas, but the preparatory tint gave her the key for the whole composition.

See "Fruit Still Life" and "Blue Door," page 73.

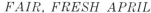

FAIR, FRESH APRIL

10. HOW TO PAINT VARIOUS PICTURE COMPONENTS

A combined knowledge of watercolor technique and the ability to analyze what one sees should enable you to reproduce almost anything on paper. In the sections to follow, there is no attempt to prescribe specific technical methods for painting all of the familiar pictorial components, but rather to suggest useful bases for your own individual analytical procedures.

HOW TO PAINT ANYTHING

There are four steps to be followed in painting any subject at all and they can be stated very simply:
1. Analyze the pattern.
2. Recognize the basic picture components, stripped of detail.
3. Reproduce those fundamentals on paper.
4. Add the details needed.

ANALYZING THE PATTERN

The great hurdle for all painting beginners is that every scene appears to be complicated by an endless assortment of detail. But most subjects, no matter how involved they seem, are basically simple. Sometimes only a very few components are required to reproduce a scene convincingly. The artist can then add as much or as little fill-in detail as he chooses. Let us analyze a subject which can be particularly confusing. The principles involved can be applied to any scene.

See "California Coast," page 71.

See The Sea, page 109.

Suppose you are at the ocean watching great combers smash against the rocks. With each surging wave the water explodes into the air, deluges the rocks, and recedes, while eddies and cascades whirl, leap, and foam, now green, now spumy white. Innumerable points of action are packed into the brief space of a few seconds. With each wave the water-distribution pattern repeats itself almost identically, the same eddies, the same shapes, the same colors, but it is never still.

Before attempting to paint, just sit, observe, analyze, and plan. Choose the exact spot and the exact moment of wave action that you want to paint. Now rule out and refuse to see all other movements of the water, concentrating on the pattern at that instant exclusively. Study the forms, colors, and values of the scene. Within ten minutes or less you will probably have memorized them. You will then be able to reproduce the subject almost as well as if it were stationary.

LIGHT AND SHADOW

The mood of a landscape picture is often established by the time of day or the weather conditions portrayed. These, in turn, affect or are affected by the way the painter handles light and shadow. The following list, combined with other special topics in this section, will suggest particular points to look for in painting subjects under special conditions of lighting or weather. In the long run, of course, you must go to nature, studying, analyzing, and memorizing the colors and values you see before you, then experimenting with your pigments until you are able to translate what you have seen to paper.

A day of bright sunlight is characterized by strong shadows. There is a great contrast of light and dark, and visibility is unlimited. In the early morning or late afternoon there are very long shadows. Most of the scene is likely to be in shadow, with just a few spots lighted by the low-lying sun. If the artist has his back to the sun, however, virtually everything will be bathed in light. "In the Shadow of the Hills" on page 152 was cast in strong light and shadow in order to turn a prosaic subject into a dramatic painting. The hills were painted in strong sepia color and the sky, which does not take up much space in the picture, was arbitrarily painted green.

See "Rhode Island Barn," page 13.

In sunrises and sunsets, with the observer facing the sun, all erect parts of the scene are seen in dark shadow and appear gray or nearly black. Little local color is visible. Level surfaces, such as grass, which are brightly lighted are darker than you might think. In fact, the whole earth is strongly contrasted against the sky. Distant parts are lighter and grayer than those near at hand.

See "Day is Done," page 93.

See Sunsets, page 105.

Billowing cloud formations usually break up the landscape into sunny and shaded expanses as the cloud shadows sweep along. With a heavy overcast, however, the whole landscape is dark and solid. There are no shadows, and objects are identifiable principally through their local colors.

See Clouds, page 104.

Moonlight gives a bluish cast to the landscape. A moonlit picture should be painted in a low key with most areas quite dark. Shadows should not be too pronounced. Study the position and angle of the moon, if it is included, for many artists take unreasonable liberties with nature and these errors are quickly detected by those who know. One artist was told his New England twilight had a Southern Hemisphere moon. Remember the crescent, or new moon, is never seen with its points down, although it has often been seen that way in pictures.

Fog usually calls for an over-all gray with virtually no whites or real darks. Receding objects quickly disappear from sight.

See Fog, page 106.

In snow scenes, the snowflakes replace the foggy mist as a softener of accents. The sky is gray, and there are no extreme darks. Most of the scene is clothed in white.

See Snowstorms, page 108.

Rain, like fog and snow, reduces distance of visibility. With rain, however, the wet surfaces of stones and other solid objects are either extremely dark or, if turned up to the sky, mirror the light. Rainy weather therefore calls for strong contrasts. Like snow, rain can be seen only against objects. Drizzly rain appears much the same as fog, except that mirror-like puddles sometimes reflect dark verticals like trees and the relatively light sky.

See Rain, page 108.

CLEAR SKIES

Clear skies are usually described as blue, but actually skies appear in all values from white to near black and in variants of all the hues of the spectrum.

No other facet of the natural scene is as variable as the sky. Not only does it change in pattern, value, and color, it also possesses a unique quality called luminosity. A clear blue sky may really be a hazy gray or violet at the horizon, ascending through a light greenish blue and increasing in depth and blueness toward the zenith. Furthermore, the sky lightens as it approaches the sun and darkens as it becomes more distant. A sky painted in flat blue without color variation is likely to appear as banal as a color postcard.

To suggest luminosity in painting a clear sky, it is necessary to contrast the sky against the scene below and to suggest vibration in the sky itself. This can be done by using two different colors, one washed over the other. Surprisingly, the effect achieved by this technique will be much more luminous or vibrant than if the same two colors are mixed beforehand and applied as a single wash.

To use this technique, first prepare two separate pans of diluted color, say blue and a warm yellow. Cobalt or any other smooth-flowing blue could be used with Yellow Ochre, Raw Sienna, or Cadmium Orange. Both colors should be thinned out with a great deal of water. Now turn the picture upside down on its slanted support and, beginning at the horizon, brush the thin yellow wash the width of the sky, continuing the wash downward to the bottom of the paper, which is, of course, the top of the picture. At the start the yellow must be very weak (no darker than linen color) and grow still weaker as the wash progresses, as more and more water is gradually added. When the wash is finished, the top of the sky will be pure white, the yellow will be deepest at the horizon and evenly graduated between the two extremes. When the yellow wash is thoroughly dry, the picture is turned upright and, beginning at the top, the blue wash is brushed in in the same manner as the yellow, weakening the hue as it descends. When the blue reaches the horizon, it must be thin indeed. With both operations completed, the result will be a luminous sky, pale greenish at the bottom and strong blue at the top. It should be emphasized by a solidly painted landscape below. The sky in "Ruddy Veteran," page 54, was painted in the manner just described. The blue wash was grayed somewhat to match in key the brilliant tree, which was also considerably neutralized.

See Autumn Colors, page 100.

CLOUDS

The great billowy puffs that course over the bright blue sky in the summer are called cumulus clouds. Their substantial thickness gives them definitely shaded bottoms and sides, except those surfaces exposed to the sun, which are approximately white. The relative positions of the individual large clouds and the directions in which they move should be carefully considered, for they are too important compositionally to be casually placed.

Cold gray nimbus clouds are rain or snow clouds. They are dense, formless masses which usually obscure the sky. If by chance there are breaks between them, one sees only the high level stratus clouds above them. Sometimes the lower nimbus clouds are broken up by wind, and the fragments, being nearer the earth than their parents, are plainly discernible as what sailors call "scud."

A nimbus cloud formation should be painted in an overall strong gray. The lighter sections can be mopped out in a deliberately planned pattern while the paint is still moist, then touched up with a brush for accents and corrections, and the whole allowed to dry. The effect will appear accidental and spontaneous. Remember that the contrasts between lights and darks are not great, but they are definite.

The cumulo-nimbus cloud is the familiar thunderhead which grows up out of a nimbus cloud layer, often to mountainous heights. It is the only cloud that might be described as of vertical formation. It appears to be built of firm cotton puffs piled one above the other, each sharply defined. Of course, a painting need not be literal. The details may be merely suggested. In analyzing the pattern of a sky, remember that the underside of a cumulus or nimbus cloud layer can be astonishingly level, appearing almost as flat as a ceiling. Like a ceiling, it should be painted upside down. The individual clouds may be thought of as great, roundish cushions in various sizes. Sketch A, Figure 50 shows a preliminary arrangement of clouds. In painting the actual picture, the regularity of the outlines would have to be broken up as in B. Notice how the shapes placed one behind the other diminish in size as they recede, the ellipses approaching more and more a straight line until, in the extreme distance, only horizontal strokes are needed to indicate the cloud field. Clouds near the horizon appear horizontal, with very little vertical dimension except for the cumulo-nimbus thunderheads which appear like mountains of solidified froth.

See "Clouds at Sunset," page 112.

See page 107.

SUNSETS

A sunset is made up of three factors: 1. The sun, if still above the horizon, or its rays, if below. 2. The clouds or atmospheric mist which intercept the rays of the sun and cause the changing color patterns. 3. The clear sky beyond the clouds.

The sky itself is virtually always the same. Close to the sun there is a creamy glow which becomes greener and then bluer as it ranges outward. If clouds or haze are absent, this is all we see. The whites and grays and the bright yellows, oranges, reds, and pinks appear only in the clouds or the vaporous mist.

The clouds float about in definite strata, those of identical formation cruising at the same level. The heights vary from ground level to perhaps six miles. The lower ones are usually the puffy cumulus clouds, seen as individuals.

As the sun retires below the horizon, shadows darken first the earth, then the low-flying clouds, and later the higher cloud layers. Between the observer and the sun, the clouds or haze provide the bright reds, which diminish in brilliance as they become more distant. The sunlit sides of clouds are white. Clouds completely in shadow are dark gray and may be seen strongly contrasted against the still sunlit, creamy, high-level clouds.

The combinations are never-ending. No two sunsets are alike, but the behavior pattern is always the same.

To paint a sunset scene, select a viewing position by the sea or on a hilltop, the higher the better. You aren't likely to see much from a valley. There must be some clouds in the western sky, and preferably haze. The most magnificent displays occur when the sky holds two vaporous layers, low-lying cumulus and very high stratus clouds. The time for observation is between twenty minutes before and twenty minutes after actual sunset. The pattern changes continually so that every three or four minutes you see a new sky.

See "Day is Done," page 93.

See "Sunset" and "Clouds at Sunset," page 112.

It may be advisable simply to study the "anatomy" of sunsets for a few nights, perhaps making quick sketches with a pencil and including notes about the colors. In that way, you can record several arrangements and paint the best one from memory and the knowledge you have gained from analytical observation. Color photographs can also be used as notes, but don't paint a watercolor copy of a photograph. In actual painting a good method is to draw arbitrarily a very low horizon line and paint the sky above it. The earth scene can be added later. Remember that the earth will appear very dark and, by contrast, its darkness will add brilliance to the colors of the sky.

Sunrise effects are similar to sunsets, but the sequence is reversed.

FOG

Fog appears in various shades of gray, some warm, some cool, but always gray, with no pure whites and no extreme darks except perhaps in the immediate foreground, and even these are grayed somewhat. All color and value differences are subtle. There are no strong contrasts. If you study and analyze fog, you will see that only the near-at-hand features show any degree of contrast and that as the other parts recede, they resolve themselves into separate flat upright planes, like stage scenery, each one grayer and lower in value than the one in front of it. Only the near planes show distinct color. The farther ones are virtually all gray. Infinity in a fog may be no more than a few hundred feet, and the whole picture has to be telescoped into that short depth. Although the regular laws of aerial perspective apply in fog scenes, distance is measured in yards instead of miles.

See "Foggy Morning," page 54.

See "Fire and Fog," page 113.

See "Winter Fog," page 114.

To paint a fog scene, I usually mix a pan of medium gray, avoiding sediment colors, and wash the mixture over the entire paper. If there are to be near-white areas in the foreground, I mop them out lightly while the paper is still wet. Then, while the color is still moist or after it has dried depending on the effect I want, I paint in the series of upright planes — usually beginning with the furthermost. This is often a gray just a trace darker than the over-all color. The planes become gradually darker and more colorful as they move forward. Near objects are painted in reasonably strong detail and color, but even here I mix some gray into every color. Working on moist paper is often advantageous, for the color applications tend to merge with the background and assure soft edges.

A

Figure 50. Preliminary layout arranged to insure proper perspective of clouds (A), and realistic development of cloud pattern (B).

B

Figure 51.

SNOWSTORMS

Painting a snowstorm is much the same as painting a fog, with snow-flakes taking the place of mist. Visibility may be a little greater and, of course, all top surfaces appear white. However, as in painting fog, there is no real white. All snow must be grayed somewhat. Everything being relative, we can judge a value only by comparing it with a standard of some sort. Nothing in nature is whiter than snow. However, if you hold up a brightly lighted white card and squint past it at a real snow storm, you will see that the snow appears to be much darker than white.

See Tricks in Watercolor, page 43.

To paint a snowstorm, cover the entire paper with a strong gray wash, then mop out the white areas and paint in the colored areas. Remember that the snow appears grayer as it recedes in the distance. If snowflakes are not indicated, either individually or by swishes of the brush, the picture may suggest mist or murk rather than storm. A few flakes can give an impression of great activity. They can be scratched out with a razor blade, or masking liquid can be applied before you begin to paint. If masking liquid is used, there are several points to remember. When the maskoid is removed, the resulting white spots may have to be grayed somewhat. Also, although we think of snowflakes as very small and all of the same size, a snowflake close to the eye may appear as large as a distant chimney. It may be necessary to paint the near flakes larger than at first seems reasonable. Remember, too, that flying snowflakes cannot be seen against a stormy sky or against the fallen snow. Place them only against color dark enough to silhouette them.

RAIN

The principles for painting fog may be followed essentially for rain scenes, but there are several special problems with rain. In a rainstorm, one sees many puddles which are, in effect, mirrors. Usually they appear very light (almost white) or very much darker than the earth around them, depending on whether they reflect the sky or some solid mass, such as trees or buildings. Remember that these puddles are mirrors, and be sure to ascertain what they reflect before you paint them dark or light. Wetness makes such things as tree trunks and rocks very dark although the wet tops of flat rocks may mirror the sky and appear very light. Thus, some foreground items may show very strong value contrast.

See The Rule of Reflection in Water, page 90.

Grayness pervades a rain scene as much as it does a fog scene. Rain-drops themselves cannot be painted, but the direction of the rain can be indicated by a few moist brushstrokes. This direction can be important to your composition, so before brushing it in be sure to choose the angle right for the picture, regardless of what you may actually see. The direction of the rain is particularly important in a painting of a torrential driving rain, for then the violence of the weather is actually the subject of the picture, and the landscape details are merely a foil to emphasize this storm.

See "Downpour," page 114.

SNOW IN SUNLIGHT

The contours of a snowy surface in sunlight can be seen only because of shadows, so shadows are a leading factor to be considered in painting a snowy, sunlit scene. Don't spread the shadows around aimlessly. Study the scene carefully and learn why they assume the positions and shapes they do. Note that the long shadow of a telephone pole, for example, reveals all the surface variations, the undulations, ruts, and ridges of the area it crosses.

See "Snow in Sunlight," page 131.

Snow shadows often appear quite blue but, as in the case of skies, one must guard against a "postcard blue" effect. A blue or violet very close to neutral gray is likely to be best, though special conditions can change the rule.

Sunlit snow in the distance may seem as white as that close by, but it is not and cannot be painted that way. To suggest the necessary atmospheric perspective, snow in the distance must be subdued somewhat by blue or violet gray.

All top snow may appear pure white, but when you notice that certain areas show definite highlights, you can see that surrounding parts are actually darker. A five per cent gray is useful in modeling sunlit snow surfaces.

White paper can be used very effectively to show brilliantly lighted snow, but it is not the only way to handle this problem. Snow can be painted in quite strong grays throughout and still seem to be white. It all depends on the relationship of values.

STILL WATER

Still water is like a horizontal mirror. To paint it, you must understand the rule of reflections. In clear water, reflected colors are slightly darker than their originals. Murky water has a color of its own — perhaps cream, brown or green — which either discolors the reflection or obscures it altogether. Still water is sometimes crossed by air currents that destroy its reflecting power in patches. These breaks, which usually appear to move horizontally from side to side, can be used to advantage as composition elements.

See The Rule of Reflection in Water, page 90.

See "Day of Rest," page 133.

THE SEA

Open water is seldom still, so definite reflections are a negligible consideration. The apparent color of salt water is determined by the sky: blue sky, blue water; gray sky, gray water. However, the sea is ordinarily much darker than the sky. The rougher the water, the darker it is likely to be. The blue or green of sea water is usually far from pure blue or green. A good deal of gray is required in the mixture. Wind, cloud shadows, distance, and other influences may cause local variations of color or value. Near-at-hand waves or rollers are green, often capped with white.

See "California Coast," page 71.

When painting the sea, don't do the whole expanse in the same color or value. There should be a gradation of tint from front to back to show the distance: darker in the foreground and lighter at the horizon, or vice versa. The eye will follow a gradation of color. Note that the sea, like the land, appears softer and more neutral in color as it recedes in the distance. The sky usually appears to be almost a continuation of the water. The values differ, of course, sometimes slightly, sometimes definitely. In any case, it

See Analyzing the Pattern, page 102.

is good practice to soften the dividing line. A hard, sharp contrast at the horizon destroys the illusion of distance.

Waves are themselves parts of larger waves, or swells, that can be indicated by horizontal swishes of color, smoother and closer together as they retreat from the eye. In heavy weather, rollers or breakers are capped with white and long stretches of spume along the shore. Some artists retain these white spaces by painting with masking fluid beforehand, but personally I find it easier to leave them white as I paint. As a rule, the whites are not really as pure as they appear and usually need a bit of softening.

Remember to keep the ocean flat. Your brushstrokes should be horizontal, never diagonal.

BOATS

See "The Boatyard," Day of Rest," "Bacochibampo Bay," "Ships in Wartime Gray," page 133.

Painting boats requires more knowledge of draftsmanship than many subjects because all the structural parts, lines, and surfaces of floating vessels seem to be curved. Even a coal or sand barge, rectilinear though it may at first appear, is well supplied with curves. These many curves, divorced from plumb and level lines, can be deceptive. Study the curves in the various paintings of boats in this book. The sketch opposite is typical. From bow to stern, the gunwales of this skiff swell outward in the waist and they curve vertically as well. Figure 51 shows this double movement, yet notice that the further gunwale is drawn with a straight line. Ships present much the same problem as small boats.

See page 107.

See "Lobster Boat," page 71.

See "Day is Done," page 93.

When boats or ships are only secondary notes in marine pictures, their lines may be simply hinted at, but close-ups of boats require a sure hand at drawing.

FOREGROUNDS

The principal action in a picture usually takes place in the middle distance, so the foreground must act as a support for and a guide into that center of interest. Despite its subordinate role, the proximity of the foreground to the viewer makes it important. The foreground must be planned as a part of the whole picture. It should support and lead into the main interest. Detail and character can be suggested in the foreground, but no details should be prominent enough to upset the planned pattern of color and shadow masses.

Using the actual subject before you, but remembering that the foreground is not important in itself but simply a guide which leads the eye to the main interest, brush in simple forms, using as large a brush as feasible. The idea is to strive for compositional pattern without detail. For example, if a diagonal direction at the lower right or a dark mass at the left is needed for the plan, it should be brushed in without hesitation. It can always be rationalized later.

Once satisfied that the foreground elements are well spaced, you can turn them into recognizable objects. A diagonal stroke may become a fence rail, a branch, a pathway, or whatever seems appropriate. A dark area may suggest a rock or the shadow of an unseen tree.

Remember that the foreground must be subdued. Detail may be sug-

LA SEGOVIANA. 21¼″ x 15½″
Courtesy Mr. and Mrs. Luis De Urzaiz.

TAMBOR DANCER. 21″ x 15″

CLOUDS AT SUNSET

SUNSET

FIRE AND FOG. 21″ x 29″

WINTER FOG

DOWNPOUR
Collection Mr. and Mrs. Hardie Gramatky

gested, but it should not be obtrusively delineated. For example, a mass of yellow grass can be painted broadly with a one-inch brush, then a few individual blades of grass can be indicated by hairlines. This can produce a surprising illusion of thousands of individual blades of grass. A bush with a singular leaf pattern might be drawn in considerable detail with a fine brush and then washed over with a flood of color while still moist. This will simplify the bush and pull it together. Most of the line drawing will be lost, but enough will remain to suggest a great deal of leafy detail.

Many types of foregrounds are shown in the paintings in this book. In "The Old Town, Gerona" on page 92, the subject has very little depth. The church and the mass of dwellings occupy most of the picture and constitute the entire middle ground. A simple foreground was needed, one that would set the buildings back a reasonable distance but still allow an unimpeded view of the houses. Grass, a tree, and small unobtrusive figures at the left fill that need.

Another kind of foreground is seen in "California Coast" on page 71. This picture is divided into three parts: the warm-colored rocks and weeds of the foreground, the gray rocks in the middle distance, and the blue-green sea in the far distance. Interest centers around the middle ground, and the foreground is a foil for it. Much unobtrusive detail is hinted at, but very little is actually delineated.

TREES

The basic rule for painting a tree is to choose a good tree, use it as a model, and paint as its color and construction suggest. On occasion, trees may be indicated with only a simple stroke of color to suggest an appropriate contour, but when individual trees are being portrayed, they must really appear to be individuals. A mass of green pigment will not suffice.

Remember there are no two trees exactly alike. They have a great range of character which is affected by species, age, environment, time of the year, and other factors. The picture should reveal all of the individual characteristics of the tree or trees shown. By cataloguing the distinguishing features, you will be able to analyze them quickly and systematically. Study the general shape, the fronds, the skeleton or framework, the base of the trunk, the age or condition, and the color.

Note the general shape of various types. There are the straight and rigid spruce and the pliant willow, the solid Norway maple, the gracefully forked elm, the twisted old apple, and all manner of types between. Which does your model resemble?

Fronds are the large leaf clusters at the ends of the branches. Do they hang down, stand erect, or extend horizontally? Are they round, pointed, irregular, closely or loosely packed? Notice that frond shapes often follow the shape of the tree itself.

Are the trunk, limbs, branches, and twigs straight or twisted, fluent or angular? How do they spring from the trunk—rectangularly or in graceful forks? Is the bark smooth, rough, or mottled?

How does the tree spring from the ground? Is it straight and clean, like a light pole, or is there an expansive root formation above ground?

Notice that young trees tend to be symmetrical, smooth, and clean while old trees are likely to be rangy, gnarled, bumpy, twisted, and scarred.

Trees run the gamut of color from the pale green of the aspen to the black green of the yew. The color of a single tree can change from yellow green in the spring through solid green in the summer to yellow, red, or brown in the autumn. Look at your model and see what color it actually appears. Don't assume it is "tree green." Notice also that the foliage of a tree in sunlight has basically only two values, those of the sunlit and shaded color; any minor variations from these two values are usually accidental. Examine the color of the trunks and branches. Are your models white birches, pale gray beech trees, scabby-looking sycamores, or another kind of tree with a trunk of some shade of brown or gray?

Many kinds of tree paintings are reproduced throughout this book. "Ruddy Veteran" and "Autumn in the Air," both in color on page 54, are portraits of individual trees. Trees are also the main subject of "Wispy Willows" on page 132, "Monterey Coast" on page 121, "In the Woods" on page 131. Trees are secondary but important elements in many other pictures, particularly "In a Provence Market" on page 2, "Winter Fog," page 114, "Family Picnic," page 93, and "The Little Statue," page 53.

IN THE WOODS

In the woods, where tree tops merge with each other, leaving no outlines, where sunlight breaks through a million apertures, and where tree trunks abound without order, the effect is utter visual confusion. Patterns that might make interesting compositions are not easily detected. It is necessary to analyze, simplify and plan. You can't paint a million leaves, but you can *suggest* them.

Using a wide, flat brush, paint the floor of the forest in local sunlit color and then brush in large masses to represent the tree tops. Next, with simple strokes, add tree trunks and other elements such as boulders or clumps of dark bushes as accents.

So far only relatively light colors, or sunshine values, have been used. Now analyze the scene's over-all sun-and-shadow pattern and boldly brush a mixture of dark warm gray pigment over some of the areas already painted. This will represent the shadow pattern.

Always keep in mind the all-important requirement of pattern. Each area should be calculatedly spaced, regardless of the actual disposition of elements in the scene. There should be a pleasing arrangement of lights and shadows, tree top colors, tree trunks, earth, rocks, sky openings, and the like, all definite enough to be judged easily. If any parts of the pattern are unsatisfactory, they should be corrected before any further painting is done.

To break up the severity of the sharply defined color shapes, correct the colors of the tree foliage in the foreground, indicate sunlit and shaded areas, paint in a few definite leaf clusters, add light and dark accents, and pick out a number of sky holes. Leaves in the middle distance should be treated as masses. Those farthest away should be subdued with a pale violet or blue wash, whether the eye sees them that way or not. Tree trunks may be separated into shaded and sunlit surfaces, if necessary. The trunks and branches near-at-hand can receive individual treatment, those in the distance may merge into the foliage. The earth may also be "loosened up" by adding in the foreground pebbles, fallen trunks, grass, dead leaf masses, or whatever details seem appropriate.

To finish the picture it is only necessary to correct tonal values and add a few accents.

It is surprising how a busy forest scene can be indicated with little color variety. Extreme simplification is the secret. By squinting through nearly closed eyes, you can learn to see the myriad details of forest foliage in a few simple values. It is rarely necessary to deviate very far.

BUILDING INTERIORS

The major factor that must be considered in painting interiors of buildings is that of the key or tonality of the scene. The volume of light inside the average house on a sunny day is less than one-fiftieth of that outside, yet the indoor objects appear to be as clearly lighted as those outside.

Ordinarily, when an artist depicts a room interior, he unconsciously raises the tonality of the lighting so that the room appears as brightly lit as an outdoor scene. This, of course, is quite proper. However, there are times when both indoor and outdoor views must be included in one picture. Such a project confounds many artists. If they continue painting the interior in a high key, there can be no value contrast between the interior and the exterior and it will be impossible to suggest sunshine in the open area.

In the picture "Barn Interior," I applied a heavy wash, probably a 30 per cent gray, over the entire drawing except for the space of the open door, a small window at the upper left, and a few chinks where sunlight enters. When dry, that dark wash was considered white and other interior values were painted relatively darker. For the area of the open door, on the other hand, the white paper rated as white. Actually I painted two pictures in one, in two different keys. When seen in color, the sun really shines on the open field and the doorway stands out with the brilliance desired.

See "Barn Interior" page 39.

Remember that, since all tonal values are relative, a very dark value can appear light and can even suggest white convincingly.

ARCHITECTURAL SUBJECTS

To paint architectural subjects accurately in any medium requires an ability to draw and a thorough knowledge of perspective. Also helpful, if one aims at "architectural portraiture," is a knowledge of architecture itself.

In the watercolor medium, there are three general ways to paint buildings. First of all, they can be painted in a fluid style in which masses are merely suggested. Or they can be painted freely but with individual buildings clearly identified and their details suggested though not delineated. Finally, they can be painted as "architectural portraits," whether of whole structures or smaller sections, with details drawn accurately or suggested with some degree of definition.

The first method is most commonly followed today, probably because "juicy" watercolors are extremely popular and also because watercolor offers a perfect means for reasonably combining structural rigidity and fluidity of appearance.

In painting city scenes, I frequently use the second method which undoubtedly represents a carry-over from my one-time practice of architectural design. The most difficult hurdle of my early painting career was that of "loosening up," of ignoring minutiae and learning simply to hint at all except the principal features. This method, which depends on the defining of form and subordination of parts, allows the artist to develop bold patterns and dramatic conceptions. "Union Square," on page 154, was painted by the second method. The third approach is exemplified by "St. Patrick's Cathedral," page 51, "Temple of Diana, Nimes," page 42, and "Church in Morelia," page 6.

See "Library Lion," page 51.

See Wet-in-Wet, page 38.

For painting city buildings, the wet-in wet method or a modification of it to suit one's individual needs is excellent. Using the widest flat brushes available, indicate entire buildings with a swish of color, allowing the edges to dry soft and making sure the pencilled outlines are not followed too closely. Shaded areas can be brushed in similarly with darker color. When the pigment is dry or nearly dry, dab in, not too sharply, indications of windows, cornices, doorways, pediments, and similar details. Line is often combined with wash very effectively in architectural subjects. Very fluidly painted architecture is usually used as a background for some nearer point of interest which is more definitely executed.

See Line and Brush, page 40.

Artists working in this apparently careless manner often begin with accurate drawings, heedfully calculated in terms of perspective. These are then used as a base for the loose brushwork, but are never allowed to show through the liquid technique.

See Perspective, page 83.

For my own work I usually prepare an accurate layout with vanishing points, horizon line, and other necessary perspective aids, though liberties are taken later with the drawing to give it a free-hand appearance. I also methodically work out a preparatory color sketch to show the spacing of shadows and the like, for these are usually more pronounced in architectural subjects than in landscapes and greater care is needed in composing them.

STILL LIFE

See "Vegetable Still Life," page 52.

See "Fruit Still Life," page 73.

Unlike most subjects, a still life can be painted with considerable verisimilitude, because the arrangement is designed in advance. The composition is worked out in the subject itself instead of on the paper. It is essential, therefore, in choosing still-life subjects to avoid the commonplace, those subjects made stale by incessant choice. If commonplace material is used, it should at least be presented in a fresh way. A still life need not always rest on a table top, nor need it be viewed always from the same old angle. Much can be learned from good photographers. Note the unusual lighting and angles of their shots. Without becoming eccentric, the painter himself can adopt similar approaches.

The foregoing suggestions apply of course to serious esthetic conceptions. For practice painting, the stress on the unusual is not so necessary.

FLOWERS

The essential characteristic of a cut flower arrangement is its irregularity or looseness, so the admonition to "loosen-up" applies with special force to flower painting. Don't try to draw every flower and leaf. Drawing should be restricted to a rough layout that shows only the placement of the bouquet and its principal divisions. Flower groups should be *painted*, not photographed. Forget the pencil. Feel your way along with the brush and liquid paint, a little lighter than you actually want so there is room for modeling and development later. Place the individual large blossoms or groups of blossoms with simple blobs of color. Don't think about petals, centers, or detail. Concentrate on pattern. Look for a pleasing design of colors whether it follows that of the subject or not. Next, add the greenery, also in loose, flat, approximate shapes arranged as you think it should be and not necessarily as it is. Think of the green as a unit rather than as a lot of stems and leaves.

See "Winter Posies," page 151.

The shadow areas of the individual parts and of the bouquet as a whole can be added next in broad flat shades. The shading of a rose, for example, might be just a single wide stroke.

The painting thus far represents the three-dimensional quality of the subject. Now you can add the detail—as much or as little as you want—but, to repeat, keep it loose. There is nothing more deadly than a cast iron bouquet. Put the background in last to set off the flowers.

PORTRAITS AND FIGURE PAINTING

Figure paintings are compositions in which figures are the main interest and all else is background or supporting material. Figure painting and especially portraiture call for greater technical skill than landscape work. A good knowledge of drawing is necessary to achieve the likeness that is essential in portraiture and the accurate definition of the anatomy that is required in figure painting. Aside from the necessity for accurate drawing, great technical command of the watercolor medium is also required. Watercolor's propensity toward accidental formation makes it a most difficult medium for portraiture and figure painting. If one is unable to achieve a likeness while retaining the freedom and fluidity expected in a watercolor, it may be better to paint these subjects in a more easily controlled medium, such as oil.

See "Tambor Dancer," and "La Segoviana," page 111; "Party Dress" and "The Sisters Lopez," page 134.

For the portrait shown on page 91, I first made a very small sketch of the head and then designed the attendant material to support it, much as I would plan a landscape. Remember that a portrait is not just a head in a rectangle. The rules of composition apply here the same as elsewhere. I wanted to paint a picture as well as a portrait. The decorative floral background was purposely included for that reason and to help show off the wetness of watercolor. In "Party Dress" on page 134 the background was so designed that the dark face, contrasted against the very light passage, becomes the focus of the viewer's attention. A watercolor portrait must be more than a likeness—it must be a *watercolor* likeness.

See "Portrait of Eileen," page 91.

FIGURES IN A SCENE

See "Moorish Gate," page 94; "Rocky Beach," page 72; "Family Picnic," page 93; "Union Square," page 154; "The Little Statue," page 53; "St. Patrick's Cathedral" and "Library Lion," page 51.

In a scene with figures, as opposed to a figure painting or portrait, the over-all subject is important and the figures are merely aspects of the composition. Such figures, therefore, must be painted in keeping with the other picture elements—loosely or carefully, as the case may be, but not as though they deserved special attention as individuals. As mentioned before, a human figure, however small, always attracts special attention and can easily "steal the show." It is necessary to watch for this.

Broadly speaking, there are three types of figures that may inhabit a scene. Figures close at hand should be drawn with enough detail to make them individuals. Figures in the middle distance can be merely suggested by indicating their dress and attitudes. Those in the distance are likely to be little more than monotone shapes.

If you are painting a scene that involves many persons, a street scene for instance, be careful not to space them too evenly or in combinations of similar size. Instead, place a group here, a few couples elsewhere, a number of individuals, and then perhaps a few really large clusters. In painting a large group of figures, think of them collectively, as units or masses, and not as a number of different people. Let the shapes or the outlines of the group take precedence over the details within it. The idea is to compose a good picture pattern, and the shapes and proper spacing of the group masses will help to do this.

See Placing Figures in a Picture, page 84.

See Sizing Figures, page 84.

Remember that in looking over a throng, you can see all the heads, but the bodies of those in the nearest ranks only. When the crowd outline is on paper, dot in the heads with a brush full of color, perhaps pink or orange. You need not show every head. A few will suggest many. Now suspend bodies from the nearest line of heads to give the crowd a vertical dimension, a front wall and an appearance of mass. If necessary, dab in color around the heads to represent hair, hats, or scarves. The white paper between the heads will probably be too conspicuous, so apply a loose wash of very pale blue or gray over the whole crowd group. The slight merging of colors that results will resolve the group into a definite unit. Nearer figures can be treated in a more individual way.

BLACK HOLES

See "Market on a Mound," page 19; "Belem Tower," page 144; "Church of San Juan, Chapultepec," page 53.

Openings into dark chambers, cave entrances, cellar doorways, and the like appear solid black, and many artists paint such areas just that way. This results in an appearance of black solidity rather than the emptiness which the holes really suggest.

See Use of Black Pigment, page 99.

To avoid this problem, swish a stroke or two of some other color—perhaps blue or green—into the thick black paint while it is still wet, then leave it to dry in only partial mixture. The color will be barely visible when dry, but the slight divergence from black will give the impression of a mysterious something within the hole that will suggest space rather than solidity. As mentioned before, a combination of two or three very dark shades used at full strength can give a more intense and vibrant dark than black alone. The impression of dark, open space is given by leaving the colors imperfectly mixed.

SHADOWS

A single large shadow may cover a number of objects of different hues, such as the side of a white house, an adjoining red shed, and a yellow blanket spread on green grass. The shadow has a cohesive influence, pulling together its member colors so they become agreeable parts of the whole. This is the essence of repose, that the whole is more important than any of its parts. The over-all gray of the shadow area brings all the colors into harmony.

See "In the Shadow of the Hills," page 152.

I have already referred to "shadow color." This is a gray which inclines toward one of the spectral colors. Ordinarily I mix gray by combining a brown and a blue, perhaps Sepia and Cobalt Blue for a dark shadow, or Raw Umber and Cobalt or Cerulean Blue for a lighter one. This shadow mixture is applied uniformly over all shaded parts of a picture, whatever their colors may be. Then, while still moist, the shadow is keyed to the color of the object it falls on by flooding in a bit of paint of the underlying hue. Where the shadow falls on white, it is diluted with a drop of water or mopped out slightly with a brush.

See Neutralized Color, page 99.

MONTEREY COAST. Courtesy of Kennedy Galleries, New York.

Because of their unusual natural growth pattern and the windy punishment they consistently receive, Monterey cypresses are quite unlike the general run of trees. In painting special trees, of any description, study their peculiarities and be sure to stress these individual characteristics.

11. ADVANCED TECHNICAL INSTRUCTION

When one is learning a new skill, there are many problems that seem not to exist at all until a certain amount of experience has been acquired. Then suddenly, after the basic technique is under control, there is likely to be a dreadful awareness of how little one knows.

In the following pages I have tried to cover some of the many and varied problems that continue to plague painters even after they have turned out a number of acceptable watercolors. Overcoming some of these problems may mean the difference between passable and successful paintings.

WORK FROM STRUCTURE TO DETAIL

The big masses or units *must* be laid out first. These are then divided into smaller parts and subdivided into still smaller portions. Finally come the details. In actual work, the painting of masses is easier for the oil painter than the aquarellist. The former can brush them in simply and directly, while the watercolorist must be more cautious because he can't paint light over dark.

It is essential to cover all parts of the paper with color (with the possible exception of the sky) at the very start. Until the picture can be seen as a whole (if only roughly), it cannot be evaluated and it is unwise to proceed to the second painting stage before the structural foundation is solid.

In applying the color, ignore the details, including minor light or white spots. Paint right over them if necessary. They can be lifted out later. As experience grows, you will learn to make allowances for them. Keep the color washes reasonably light, so they can be changed if necessary and so lights can be mopped out. Light washes are much more easily lifted than dark ones. The whole picture can be assessed as easily in a light key as in a dark key, but one must have the whole color plan on paper before it can be judged at all.

When the large masses are correctly arranged, divide them into smaller ones and finish the painting, but take care that the work on the smaller units does not destroy the identity of the larger ones. This rule must be followed no matter how much you subdivide. An experienced artist may cut many corners, carrying a good part of the painting conception in his mind. He may be less methodical, planning less on paper, even finishing whole sections of a picture before starting others. But until one has developed such ability it is better to follow a step-by-step procedure.

DON'T BE AFRAID TO LOSE THE DRAWING

Paintings are not colored drawings. A painting must be executed in masses of color, not in line. The preliminary pencil drawing should accurately show the placement of the various parts and their general shape, but not the fine detail. One must assume that the pencil lines will be lost once the color application begins. Whatever detail is to be depicted can be added after the large areas of color have been satisfactorily established. It can be drawn in, correctly but not stiffly, with a fine brush, using a very thin and sketchy line. The advantage of drawing with paint is that after a wash of water or color is added, or the color areas are manipulated a bit, the lines merge with the general color, leaving a delightful suggestion of detail but without hard delineation.

THREE-VALUE SYSTEM

In nature there are innumerable values of light and dark. The beginner often assumes that he should try to reproduce all of them, but the reverse is true. Simplification—elimination of the superfluous—is one of the foundations of great art.

Virtually anything can be reproduced realistically and acceptably on paper or canvas with only three values: a light, a medium, and a dark. Many teachers have built their instruction methods around a three-value system which is applied not only to objects within a picture, but to the composition as a whole. The system works out well, but since most pictures have many colors, and thus make the judging of values difficult, it may be more easily comprehensible if you simply apply the three-value rule to each component of your picture as you paint it. The net over-all result will closely approximate the three-value ideal.

The medium value might be called the local color of the object painted. Theoretically, you should begin by painting that value, later adding the highlights and the darks. However, in transparent watercolor, where it is necessary to work from light to dark, you may want to start with the light value. Of course it is possible, even in watercolor, to apply the medium value first, mopping out the highlights with a thirsty brush, a cloth, or a sponge while the color is still wet.

The paintings of the torsos (Figure 52) show how a limited number of values can describe an object three-dimensionally. To make the appearance more interesting, edges may be softened and an accent added here or there, but basically there are only three values.

See page 124.

RANGE OF VALUE

Pictures painted in full chiaroscuro should have a spread of value from virtual white to black, and paintings in lower key should range between a relatively bright light and a dark. Even one definite light or dark touch will add life to a composition. The strongest light and the strongest dark should be near the center of interest. Don't place strong lights or darks near the corners or edges.

A

B

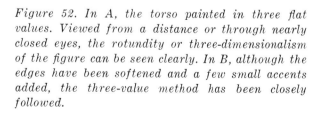

Figure 52. In A, the torso painted in three flat values. Viewed from a distance or through nearly closed eyes, the rotundity or three-dimensionalism of the figure can be seen clearly. In B, although the edges have been softened and a few small accents added, the three-value method has been closely followed.

THE IMPORTANCE OF EDGES

Examine closely the paintings of old masters and you will notice in many that while certain areas are executed in virtually flat color and value, the edges of those areas, especially the shadows, show infinite variety, ranging all the way from soft and indefinite to hard and crisp as they lose and find themselves, sharply separating two areas here and softly merging them there. Unless you are painting a poster, edges should not be too clear-cut. They can be shown quite strong and contrasty around the more important parts of the picture with soft transitions in the minor divisions.

PAINT THE SKY FIRST OR LAST?

The majority of watercolor landscape artists paint skies first. The sky is generally lighter than the earth and, in theory at least, it can be difficult to paint the lighter area around or over the darker parts. Personally, however, I find it more satisfactory to leave the sky until the last unless I know at the start exactly the kind and intensity of sky needed. Often one is not sure of that point in advance.

Naturally, the sky and the earth must be calculated and painted to complement each other. You cannot arbitrarily insert any sky that appeals to your fancy nor reproduce the one apparent at the moment simply because it is there. The upper and lower parts of the picture must harmonize and must respectively contribute whatever is needed to bring the whole picture into balance.

It is easier to key the sky to the landscape than the reverse, for often the sky calls for little more than a simple wash effect, while the landscape proper can be relatively complicated. If you wonder how it is possible to paint a sky down to the trees and housetops without showing a hard division or without loosening the pigment already applied, the answer is that if a picture is loosely painted it doesn't matter if the earth-sky line is irregular. If a smooth effect is wanted, the sky wash may be extended over a part of the already painted earth without harm, provided it is done with a single swish of a large brush, which is lightly and loosely applied, then left alone to dry. Don't try a second stroke in the same place, for it will surely dislodge the underlying pigment—but you are allowed *one* try. Any change in the landscape painting which may result can easily be corrected after the sky color is thoroughly dry.

THIN WATERCOLORS

Unless one is experienced, he is likely to paint thin watercolors. In the first place, watercolor pigment always becomes lighter as it dries. A few minutes practice matching dried color samples with liquid watercolor will show how much extra pigment must be applied to get the dry effect required. Second, colors in nature seem to appear lighter than they are. Usually the true depth of color of any area can be ascertained only by comparing it with a lighter area, such as the sky. The experienced painter learns to make allowances for these illusions.

Transparency in watercolor is certainly desirable, but a landscape should resemble earth first and pigment second. There is nothing transparent about the earth. A picture of it should suggest substance. From time to time, under different weather conditions, squint at the horizon and you will see that the earth is virtually always darker than the sky, even when the sky may be said to be "black." The sky is usually the source of light, whatever the quality of the day, and only under unusual conditions can anything on land be lighter than that.

See Vivid Greens, page 100.

Naturally, a sunlit field of green grass and brown earth appears light in color. Yet it is astonishing how dark a green can be used for sunlit grass. Painted sunlight depends not upon lightness of color, but upon the strong contrast between lights and shadows. The shadows may have to be painted very dark.

LOOSENESS IN WATERCOLOR PAINTING

Looseness, or a suggestion of fluidity, is the principal charm of watercolor painting and the quality that distinguishes it from other mediums. Looseness is achieved by apparent carelessness, by using the largest brushes the occasion will permit to administer fluid pigment directly, leaving it to dry in "accidental" poolings without further meddling. Precise outlines, delineation, and fussy brushing are avoided. Sometimes one passage at a time is built up and completely finished while still moist, then left alone to dry.

There is, however, another side to this matter. Many pictures are spoiled because the painter confuses sloppiness or looseness of planning with looseness of brushing. A fixation on loose painting can prevent one from learning to organize his work. Let me emphasize that looseness in watercolor applies only to the application of color. Rules of composition remain unchanged. Though the expert may handle his medium freely, underneath his apparently unstudied movements there is a very definite pattern of which he never loses sight.

See Planning the Picture, page 25.

Before you can paint loosely, you must know how to plan tightly. This planning can best be done in a very small sketch. Littleness dictates simplification, and the pattern can be sharply defined like a poster. The more the artist intends to lose himself in unrestricted brushing, the more valuable the sharp pattern will be. Only when you know the fundamentals are you able to improvise.

TEXTURE

Many kinds of textures are encountered in nature, and reproducing them on paper is an important part of watercolor technique. In addition to their usefulness in representing the surface or "feel" of objects pictured, textures are valuable in adding variety to a picture, for we don't want all surfaces alike.

There are textures of things and textures of painting. There are the foamy wetness of ocean waves, the rounded smoothness of pebbles on the beach, the dried out grain of an old wood plank. Peeling paint, polished silver, mossy rocks, ragged tree bark, old brick walls, a kitten's fur—these are only a few of the hundreds of textures that one may wish to represent.

Only practice and experience can tell you how to achieve all the effects

A

B

Figure 53. The shadows in A were painted in life-less color. In B the shadows have been made luminous by adding a suggestion of detail.

127

you will want, but sometimes they may be easier than you expect. Waves sparkling in the sunlight, for instance, can be suggested with horizontal strokes of a half-dry brush that leave the white grain of the paper exposed. To simulate wood grain perfectly, use a wide flat brush lightly charged with color and drag it unevenly along the paper. On the other hand, the reproduction of the inherent texture of some things, such as an ancient shingled roof or a wet, slick mud flat, may demand more careful analysis and may require serious painting and color modeling.

Textural effects of the paint itself can also add a great deal of variety and interest to a painting. This kind of texture can be achieved in a score of ways. Among the most common are drybrushing in various directions, smudging, spattering, scraping with a knife or using a razor blade broadside, or dabbing with a crumpled cloth or tissue.

See Drybrush Painting and Palette Knife Painting, page 40; Razor Blade and Pocket Knife, page 47.

Unusual textures can also be achieved by taking advantage of the sedimentary colors which have a tendency to granulate or settle. They create a pebbled effect somewhat like morocco leather when washed onto rough paper because the surface depressions encourage the minute pigment particles to collect.

See Sedimentary and Dye Colors, page 23.

Cerulean Blue, Cobalt Violet, and most of the earth colors are very good for this purpose. Mixtures of sedimentary colors, such as Cerulean Blue with Umber or Indian Red often create a more definite pebbled pattern than any one color alone. Experiment will show you which are most suitable for any particular effect. You can help the granulation process by flooding the colors or mixtures over the desired areas and tilting the paper in different directions so the color can run first one way and then another before settling down to dry.

LUMINOUS SHADOWS

The lugubrious shadows often seen in watercolors are usually painted with a flat gray or near gray color, and the shadow color bears no relation to the sunlit color. One will see, for instance, a yellow house with its shadow side a cold gray when it should be a yellowish gray. This flatness and lack of color makes the shadows appear lifeless.

Any shadow, no matter how dark, can be made to look luminous by adding a few bold strokes of an even darker shade to it, especially on its borders, leaving most of the original shadow untouched. The combination of lighter and darker values within the shadow suggest detail to the observer, hence a degree of luminosity. The painting "In the Shadow of the Hills" on page 152 includes an interesting example of this. Although the shadow on the end of the foremost house was painted with exceptionally heavy color, it is quite transparent because of the even heavier accents it contains. A dash of local color flooded into the moist shadow color and allowed to dry in accidental formation can also be helpful. See A and B, Figure 53.

See page 127.

PULLING A PICTURE TOGETHER

A successful picture may include imperfect drawing and unrealistic colors, but unless the values of the color masses are right it will lack repose, a prime essential for any satisfying naturalistic picture. Repose in a picture

A

Figure 54.

B

means that each part stays in its appointed place. The important features attract the eye; subordinate factors remain subordinate; distant things stay in the distance; water lies flat, and so forth. The antithesis of repose is "jumpiness." One cannot long tolerate a "jumpy" picture.

See page 129.

Picture A, Figure 54, represents a beginner's painting. Each detail by itself is satisfactorily indicated, but the masses neither hold together individually nor separate themselves from each other. The values are not correctly related so the picture has no coherence. Its instability would soon irritate a constant viewer.

Picture B, Figure 54, shows the same scene after being "pulled together." Notice that by darkening and unifying the ends of the two houses and by reducing the sharpness of detail in the sunlit spaces, a pleasing pattern has been created, giving the picture a third dimension and producing over-all repose. Each part now assumes its proper position in the picture. The figures come forward, the tree recedes and is no longer confused with the clouds and the chimney, and the dormer becomes a recognizable architectural unit. Notice also that detail is easily seen in the shaded as well as the lighted areas, but in neither case are the details so prominent that they upset their respective color masses. Despite its division into detail, each color mass, light or dark, is still identifiable as a unit.

The cohesion and repose shown in this painting were achieved by working on each mass individually. In a light area this means the lightening of any lines or strokes that are so dark as to stand out unduly; in a dark area, it means the darkening of passages whose lightness is too noticeable. In watercolor, an already painted mass can often be pulled together by simply flooding a wash over it, details and all. If the area is light, clear water may be enough. The colors will run together slightly, making the darker details lighter and the light parts a trifle darker, thus reducing the contrast within the mass and making it a unit. For dark masses, a wash of warm gray shadow color might be used to attain the same end.

See Lightening the Value of
Dried Color, Darkening a
Passage or Changing Its
Hue, page 50.

See Neutralized Color, page 99.

I have stressed the pulling together of masses, but of course the picture as a whole must also be pulled together. This is achieved by strengthening or subduing individual masses that are out of line, by giving areas warmer or cooler tones if needed, or by using a brighter or weaker color here and there. When each of the color masses is perfectly adjusted, they will all assume their intended places and the picture will have repose.

TO MAKE THE DISTANCE RECEDE

In a picture that shows great depth of distance, it is important not only to make the distance recede, but also to be sure that the distance remains distant, that is, does not appear too lively or prominent. This is accomplished, of course, by appropriate use of linear perspective, atmospheric perspective and the perspective of detail, but there are several little tricks that may also help.

See Perspective, page 83.

Think of the landscape as a series of painted theatrical set pieces placed one behind the other. Register them in your picture in successively lower keys as they recede. Get a feeling of space between them.

SNOW IN SUNLIGHT

IN THE WOODS

WISPY WILLOWS. 15¼″ x 21¼″

WEEDS. 13¾″ x 19¼″

DAY OF REST

THE BOATYARD.
Courtesy Kennedy Galleries, New York.

BACOCHIBAMPO BAY

SHIPS IN WARTIME GRAY.
Collection Mr. and Mrs. Reginald N. Webster.

THE SISTERS LOPEZ. 26½″ x 20¾″

PARTY DRESS. 21¼″ x 15½″

TOLEDO LANDMARK. 20¾″ x 26½″
Courtesy Grand Central Art Galleries, Inc., New York.

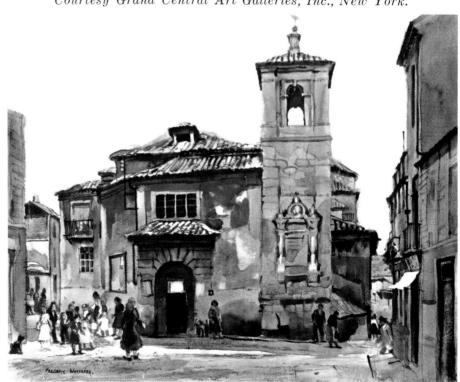

Contrast light areas against dark ones or dark areas against light ones to separate them and suggest space between them.

Use figures or objects of known size, such as houses, in diminishing sizes to show increased distance from the observer.

Place something across the horizon in the foreground or middle ground to make the horizon appear distant.

TIPS ON FINISHING A PICTURE

If you have gone as far as you feel you can with a picture and it still seems lifeless, check it against this list of faults which are typical of most watercolorists' early work.

1. Colors too thin.
2. Landscape not dark enough in relation to the sky.
3. Insufficient contrast between lights and shadows.
4. Edges too sharp.
5. Shadows dead, without luminosity.
6. Masses don't hold together.
7. Distant areas too lively.

See Thin Watercolors, page 125; Paint the Sky First or Last?, page 125; Three-Value Systems, page 123; Range of Value, page 123; Importance of Edges, page 125; Luminous Shadows, page 128; Pulling a Picture Together, page 128; Work from Structure to Detail, page 122; To Make the Distance Recede, page 130.

The cures for most of these shortcomings are discussed in the preceding pages. Reread those that apply and try to figure out where you have gone astray. One or two minor changes may make a great difference in the finished painting.

TO TAKE THE BULGE OUT OF PAPER

When a watercolor is finished, the paper is often buckled. To remove the undulations, moisten the back of the picture until it is thoroughly limp, being careful that the water doesn't creep around to the painted side. When the moisture has dried enough so that the paper is fairly dry to the touch but still flaccid, place the picture under heavy pressure and leave it until *thoroughly* dry. This may take several days. The paper will emerge completely flattened.

I paint on 400 lb. A.W.S. paper. Because of its thickness and strength it takes a good deal of wetting and a long time to dry. To soak it I place it face down on a carton somewhat smaller than the paper. When wet, the edges curl downward and shed all surplus water, leaving the painted side dry. To press it, I place the limp painting between corrugated paper boards (which allow aeration) and lay them on the floor. A specially made 24 x 32 inch board with two handles is placed over them with several gallon bottles of water on top of the board for weights. I can flatten five or six pictures at one time this way.

Buckled paintings can also be flattened by stretching. Lay the painting face down on the board, moisten the back, and after waiting a while to allow the paper to expand, seal the edges to the board with gummed paper or wide masking tape. When the paper is thoroughly dry and taut, cut it from the board or peel off the masking tape. If gummed paper has been used, it will be necessary to leave the strip adhering to the back of the picture.

In stretching paper to flatten a finished work, one need not be as thorough

See How to Stretch Paper, page 14.

as when stretching it for painting. The paper need not be so thoroughly soaked (usually a light moistening is enough) and, since the contraction will then be less, the sealing tape need not be as strong or heavy. The larger the paper, the thicker the paper, or the greater amount of soaking, the greater will be the pull as the paper contracts in drying. One should experiment, therefore, to see just how strong a sealing tape is needed for a given job. Small thin papers can be stretch-flattened with a masking tape sealed edge, but the larger or thicker papers will call for heavy gummed paper sealing.

ARTISTS' COLORS—HOW LONG WILL THEY LAST?

Many artists assume that all colors made by reputable houses or colors that are "expensive" are consequently permanent. Nothing could be further from the truth. None of the leading manufacturers claim that all their colors are fast. Some of our most exquisite and most easily manipulated hues are of a fugitive nature. It is not necessary that all colors be permanent. For certain purposes—paintings for commercial reproduction, for instance—colors of temporary durability are quite acceptable.

The permanency of colors has relatively little to do with their manufacturing source. There is no great secret to the making of standard paints and most manufacturers follow the same procedures. Artists' paints, for the most part, are little more than raw dry color well mixed with a binder, such as gum arabic for watercolor, a casein glue for casein paints, and an oil mixture for oil colors. Naturally, there are different degrees of excellence in the materials used and of care employed in grinding or mixing, but basically the lasting quality of the paints depends upon the kind of raw pigment in the mixture. Commercial paint manufacturers do not make the raw powdered pigments. They buy them, and they all buy from similar or comparable sources.

Most paint manufacturers mark their colors as Absolutely Permanent, Reasonably Permanent, or Non-Permanent. Some issue printed material telling of the source and quality of their pigments. One might feel that "permanent" cannot be qualified, that anything "permanent" is necessarily "absolutely permanent." However, "Reasonably Permanent" means permanent under ideal conditions and "Absolutely Permanent" means permanent under all normal conditions. For example, certain colors are permanent if protected from sunlight or if kept in chemically pure surroundings, but may fade in bright sun or if exposed to the chemical fumes often encountered in the atmosphere of industrial areas. Pure ultramarine, derived from lapis lazuli, is one of the most durable of colors. It is Absolutely Permanent. Yet a drop of lemon juice will destroy it immediately.

Most earth colors, which are made from pulverized soil or clay, are Absolutely Permanent. Even in strong sunlight they seem never to change. Earth colors include ochres, siennas and umbers, the Mars colors from yellow to violet, Terre Verte, etc. Other Absolutely Permanent popular colors are the cobalts, the cadmiums, the chromium oxides (Viridian, etc.), and the iron oxides (Indian Red and Venetian Red).

Pigments are derived from a wide range of diversified material which includes ground insects (Carmine), burned bones (Ivory Black), extract of roots (Rose Madder), coal tar material, and any number of mineral derivatives. Because of this, it has been found that certain colors cannot be mixed satisfactorily. Chemical action takes place through combination, and this gradually affects the color. For instance, pigments with a copper base, such as Malachite Green, may tend to blacken if mixed with the cadmium sulphides, such as the cadmium yellows and oranges. Certain chromates, such as Chrome Yellow, should not be mixed with organic colors made from vegetable or animal sources. Many color manufacturers supply leaflets which give detailed information on the forbidden combinations.

During recent years, some manufacturers have replaced certain of the old formulas with synthetic colors, or they have added the synthetic product to the old line. Emerald Green, for instance, in its pure state is aceto arsenite of copper, and as such should not be combined with Cadmium Yellow. In some brands, however, Emerald Green is now a mixture of two other standard colors, a blue and a yellow. If this synthetic color is used, the taboo is removed. Many of the new colors are aniline or coal tar products and, being of a more homogenous nature, may be mixed with each other without danger. Some of the synthetic colors are said to be Absolutely Permanent, but they have not been in use long enough to be completely trustworthy. Some of the aniline or coal tar colors are certainly not permanent or otherwise desirable.

In my own work, I use only colors that are Absolutely Permanent, with one exception. That exception is Alizarin Crimson, which I use infrequently and very sparingly. There is no Absolutely Permanent crimson or rose red pigment. Often, when a passage calls for crimson, I use Cadmium Red with Cobalt Violet added. This makes a beautiful hue, but it is not the same as crimson, nor does it have the brilliance of crimson or of carmine.

Although it might seem advisable to list here all standard colors, noting their degrees of permanency and their chemical compatibility—or lack of it—with other colors, developments in the color industry have been so rapid in recent years that it would be difficult to offer factual statements that would apply to given colors made by different manufacturers. If your artist supply store does not have printed material available on the colors it sells, write directly to the maker of your favorite brand of pigments for the latest information about his products.

SWING YOUR BRUSHES HORIZONTALLY

If you want your fields to lie flat, your clouds to resemble a ceiling, and all to recede properly into the distance, be sure your brushwork is primarily horizontal. Why? Remember that when you paint a flat or nearly flat surface such as the earth, you place the nearest things at the bottom of the paper and as the terrain recedes into the distance you show it higher and higher so that the horizon is drawn nearer the top of the paper than any other portion of the earth. From the bottom of the paper to the horizon may measure only 10 or 12 inches, but that may represent 10 or 12 miles of terrestrial distance.

Again, a flat disk such as a phonograph record is a perfect circle when

A   **B**

Figure 55. In A, the river doesn't lie flat and landscape stands on end. The river in B lies flat because of horizontal direction of brushstrokes.

viewed from directly above, but as the observer's eye is changed in relation to it, it may seem an ellipse or even a straight line. In other words, the apparent distance from front to back gets shorter and shorter, although the dimension from side to side does not change at all.

When painting a round lake two miles in diameter, you might use the entire width of your paper to indicate the two-mile left-to-right measurement and no more than an inch for the distance from the near to the far edge. If the latter distance were increased to two inches on the paper, the apparent width of the lake would double. One inch of paper represents two miles of lake! This is why it is necessary to restrain your urge to paint vertically and keep your brush strokes horizontal when depicting receding distances. Brush from side to side, letting the horizontal strokes come closer and closer together as they move into the distance. This will prevent lakes from standing uncomfortably on end. The two river scenes in Figure 55 illustrate this point.

The rules governing the painting of flat terrain apply equally to clouds. Clouds nearest the observer may be shown round and in detail, but as the artist works toward the horizon his strokes should become increasingly level.

See Clouds, page 104.

Practice that left-to-right swing. Moving sideways is the only way to travel into the distance in watercolor.

HOW WET THE COLOR?

The expert watercolorist can sense the exact degree of liquidity needed in his colors for handling a given passage, and with his brush he is able to gather up color of the precise density required. This is an indispensable skill, and it comes only from practice. It cannot be taught, but to become aware of it is an important step.

Some of the most effective watercolor work is achieved by painting one moist color into another. At times really wet color is flooded into a wet area so it will spread widely. At other times half-moist colors are applied in a really wet area to produce limited spreading. To achieve soft-edged definition, pasty color can be brushed into half-moist color. It is even possible to paint sharp detail within the area if the paint on the paper is in a state of pasty wetness and the brush color is even thicker, almost as it comes from the tube.

See Wet-in-Wet, page 38.

The beginner almost invariably applies the brush color too wet, because watercolor always appears darker wet than dry. A half hour of practice painting wet-into-wet in different stages of fluidity until the precise result desired is achieved should save him much time and chagrin when it comes to actually using the technique in painting a picture. The secret in most cases is to keep the brush color thicker than the paper color and to mix all colors heavier than one thinks is needed, but only practice can help you find the exact answer each time.

PAINTING FROM MEMORY

In a way all pictures are painted from memory, for naturally we cannot look at both the subject and the painting at the same time. We paint what we remember having seen a moment ago. But it is wise to test the memory for longer periods. You might try working in one room with your model or subject in another. Scrutinize the model only when absolutely necessary. At first you may remember little of what you have seen. However, when you find yourself balked, you will quickly be reminded of the points you should have observed.

It is surprising how quickly practice sharpens the powers of perception, teaching you to separate the trivia from the essentials and to remember the latter. Eventually, you work very largely from memory, needing only the briefest kind of memo for inspiration. This ability is necessary if you are to paint original pictures and not mere reproductions of what you see. Remember that the natural scene is to be used only as a foundation for your painting.

In practicing painting from memory, one should search not only for shapes, colors and values, but also for the over-all quality that inspired him to choose the subject—a mood, an unusual light effect, or whatever it was. It is more important to capture the aspects of the subject that contribute to this distinguishing quality than other factual details which may be of little interest in this respect.

When painting a local landscape, I usually make a small pencil sketch of the actual scene, revising it in my mind to form a good composition and making mental notes of colors and values. I return to the studio to paint the picture through the next-to-last stage, then take the painting to the scene for a final comparison, and return home again to finish the work back in the studio.

The ability to observe and analyze comes as second nature after continued practice. Painting from memory is the key to this important skill.

DISTORTION IN PAINTING

Distortion in painting may result from simple carelessness or inability to draw, or it may be done on purpose for one of many reasons. It is often used for emphasis in advertising and for comic effect in cartoons. Sculptors and muralists, on the other hand, use distortion to overcome visual illusion. Bronze or stone figures must be made considerably more bulky than their human models. Michelangelo's distorted figures on the Sistine Chapel ceiling, intended to be seen from below, are outstanding examples of effective mural distortion.

Painters commonly exaggerate to augment the force of their compositions. Exaggeration in watercolor is most useful for strengthening key features. Except where faces and figures are involved, distortion can often pass without notice. A house can be tilted, twisted, or otherwise caricatured, for example, and still appear reasonably recognizable. So one should not hesitate to exaggerate the size, shape, strength, color, or angles of any part of a picture if the over-all composition will be improved.

TOO MANY INTERESTS IN A PICTURE

Looking over a landscape for a painting subject, a beginner tends to see a lot of interesting details that he feels must go into his painting. He may put an attractive white house on the left, a big red silo and barn on the right, and some rather interesting flowers in the foreground. If, as he is likely to do, he stresses each item in detail, the picture blows apart. It has too many dominating features and thus lacks cohesion.

See Composition, page 56.

A successful picture cannot include competing themes. Of course it is possible to include a number of features in a painting, but *one* must be dominant. In composing a picture, start with the feature that interests you most, and then add, one by one, other parts of the scene to support that feature. Remember that your secondary favorites must play a subordinate role to the principal. That means they cannot be stressed and must be mercilessly discarded if they don't help to support the principal feature.

Once you have decided upon the mood for your picture and have laid out the general color scheme and the main pictorial interests, you are no longer master of the situation. You become the servant of the composition and you must give that composition what it demands, not what you may think you would like to include.

If you are in love with the white house, the red silo and barn, and the flower patch, make three separate pictures, each one featuring one of the themes.

SKETCH NOTES AND QUICKIES

The value of making quick and frequent sketches cannot be over-emphasized. In their formative days at least, most successful painters made sketch notes whenever a suitable subject and the opportunity permitted. There is no better way to perceive the structure of things, to learn to see and appreciate, and to build up a store of visual memories for later use.

All you need for sketching is a pencil or pen, fountain, ballpoint or felt-nib, and a sketchbook or pad. Watercolor sketching, though it calls for a little more preparation, affords wonderful practice and can provide valuable color memos.

Quickies are another form of rapid sketch which are employed more for technical practice than for the recording of things or events. Make a practice of painting small impressions of scenes, objects or figures with the brush, making no preliminary pencil layout and allowing only a few minutes per sketch. This practice will sharpen your perception, loosen your style unbelievably, and encourage a bold approach that is difficult to acquire using methodical procedures.

TO CHECK ON THE SUCCESS OF A PAINTING

There comes a time when even the most experienced artist cannot decide whether his picture is good or bad. He detects no positive fault, yet he dislikes the whole without quite knowing why. Every painter has noticed he can recognize the mistakes of another's work more readily than his own. He views his fellow artist's picture as a completed work and judges it with a fresh, clear mind, whereas he has followed his own composition through every bothersome detail until his mind is jaded and confused.

One remedy is to put the composition away until the travail it caused is forgotten, perhaps for a week or a month. When it is brought out again the fault will often be readily apparent. Sometimes I place a questionable picture where I must pass it occasionally. I glance at it only casually as I go by, but usually, within a few days, the answer will suddenly emerge.

PAINTING SUBJECTS ARE EASILY FOUND

Although it may call for a high degree of ability to turn some subjects into satisfactory paintings, almost anything will do. One artist-teacher, challenged to find and paint a subject within the room his class occupied at the time, painted a delightful watercolor of the students' coat rack and the varicolored clothes hanging on it.

See Choosing a Subject, page 24.

An artist who disliked the scene his friends selected for a sketching party made an excellent, full-size painting of a single large weed. In fact, weeds are the subject of two paintings reproduced in this book. A patch of growing weeds is shown on page 132 and a bouquet of dried sprays of weeds picked in December is the subject of "Winter Posies" on page 151. Another unusual subject is the picture of cemetery headstones in "Far From the Madding Crowd" on page 20. "Aquarium," on the same page, is the kind of subject that could well be right in front of you while you are wishing you could get out to the country to paint.

When kept indoors by the weather, I have sometimes selected a doll from Mrs. Whitaker's international collection and backed it with a potted geranium or some other object to show scale. Two of these paintings, "Tambor Dancer" and "La Segoviana" are on page 111.

Panoramic landscapes and other complicated subjects may be excellent picture material, but a simple doorway, a single tree, a few rocks, a shell, or any of a thousand commonplace things can also provide material for a satisfactory picture.

PRACTICE AND PERSISTENCE

To become an artist, one must practice. It is possible to learn a great deal by reading, listening, and watching others, but to develop a mental and manual dexterity that will operate without conscious prodding, there is no substitute for working yourself.

Practice drawing and painting whenever possible. At other times practice analysis of scenic material, choice of subject, observation of moods, color relations, and the like. This requires no physical equipment but can be of inestimable value when you begin a painting. In addition, you will see and enjoy many beauties that previously went unnoticed. Remember, there is more to painting than the application of pigment. Observation and analysis are perhaps even more important.

Don't discard a picture as soon as it appears unpromising. One can never really develop any composition if all are discarded at an early stage. Even though a painting may seem hopeless, keep at it until you have tried every way you can think of to improve it. Many pictures can be saved that way, but even if yours does prove hopeless, you will have gained worthwhile experience.

Don't become discouraged if some pictures are failures. Even the best artists are forced to admit defeat on paintings over which they have sweated and agonized. Actually, we learn little from our easy successes. Every success is built on a series of failures. Most progress is achieved through making mistakes, provided we don't make the same one twice.

PAINT INDOORS OR OUT?

There is no right or wrong answer to this question. One artist may enjoy an outdoor routine, while another prefers to work indoors. Many artists do both. If you restrict yourself to painting outdoors only, your work may tend to be too literal, even "photographic." The outdoor painter runs the risk of including in his pictures many unnecessary factors simply because they are there before his eyes. This is a real danger. There is much more to picturemaking than simply reproducing nature. The artist must contribute something of his own — a mood, a dramatic presentation, perhaps an original color combination — and this is extremely difficult while face to face with the scene itself. The studio habitue, on the other hand, may get into an indoor rut and thus miss, in his work, the charm and spirit of the real outdoors.

Many successful artists paint some complete pictures outdoors, others work entirely in the studio, and still others paint in the studio from sketches and notes made in the field. The latter method is especially popular because on-the-spot sketches can be developed to a point where the essence of the scene and its most interesting elements have been recorded. Later, in the quiet of the studio where the artist is free from the distraction of assertive natural details, the essential elements can be recombined to produce an effective composition.

Good representative art is a mixture of fact and fancy. It is useful to go to nature for inspiration and for the facts, but the studio may be the best place to interpret and transform them.

PAINT COMFORTABLY

Painting is exacting enough without the needless irritation of physical discomforts and other hazards, so make yourself as comfortable as possible and have your gear in order and arranged conveniently before beginning to work. The paper should be *fastened* in some way to a drawing board or other rigid surface. You can't concentrate on painting when the paper is sliding about or curling up into a roll. It's a good idea to use a board one inch longer and wider than the paper. This allows a half-inch margin of drawing board on all four sides. If your paper is larger than your board, the paper will extend loosely outward in all four directions. Such a sloppy set-up becomes a nuisance.

If thumbtacks are used, there should be enough of them and they should all be pushed in firmly. If you use only one or two tacks or insert the points lightly, the wet paper will curl eventually and eject the tacks. Tacks are usually unsatisfactory in unstretched paper anyway. As the paper expands from moisture, the tacks interfere with the movement and the paper buckles. Large clamps are better. They can be opened occasionally to accommodate the paper's expansion.

When using stretched paper, be sure the edges adhere firmly. Even if the paper comes loose at only one point, the paper tension will be lost and unevenness in the painting will result.

If you are working out of doors, try to keep the paper shaded. Bright sun on white paper will strain the eyes. Also, the colors in your picture are likely to appear drab when viewed indoors.

WEARING SUNGLASSES WHILE PAINTING

When painting outdoors, it is sometimes hard to avoid the glare of bright sunlight on the paper. This can seriously strain the eyes if they are unprotected. It is also undesirable because such a picture will appear flat when viewed indoors unless the artist knows how to compensate for the effect of the glare.

Umbrellas are impractical. Like many artists, I sometimes use dark glasses, which brings us to the question: "Don't sunglasses change the colors?" Naturally they do, but the disadvantage is not as great as it may seem, for they change in similar degree both the appearance of one's pigments and the subject itself. If the artist uses a green pigment that matches the green of a tree before him, the two greens should, theoretically at least, match also when viewed without sunglasses. There may be a slight deviation, but it usually is not enough to cause concern and one can easily correct the errant colors or values in the studio.

BELEM TOWER

The center of interest in this rather dramatic composition is a large dark spot, the heavily shaded rectangle near the center. This has been surrounded by four dark window openings and the shaded section at the lower right to steal some of its importance and prevent too-insistent concentration on it. Notice the surface texture and the airiness of the dark apertures.

12. THOUGHTS ON PAINTING

Painting is not a purely technical matter. It is not enough to paint a likeness of an object, or a scene, or a person. A camera, after all, might do as good a job or better. The purpose of painting is to create a work of art. In the beginning, of course, it is unlikely that many — or perhaps any — of one's works will qualify, but that is the goal. In the following pages, we discuss some aspects of the creative side of painting.

ORIGINALITY

Originality is a personal way of seeing things. It may be apparent in the choice of subject, a method or approach, a viewpoint, a handling of color, a style of painting, or in some other way.

Originality may stem from a lack of knowledge or experience, an innocent eye as evidenced in the work of children; from a visionary or rhapsodic nature that feels rather than calculates; or from analytical thought. Most of the great masters in all the arts, Leonardo, Michelangelo, Beethoven, and Wagner among them, possessed minds of great calculative ability, but there have also been a number of great ones in the second category, the visionaries who worked more by instinct. Van Gogh, Modigliani, and Chopin, for example.

We are not children, so we cannot honestly paint as primitives. We need not think too much about being original, but we should study ourselves and look inside for inspiration. If we do our own thinking, ignore what others would make us accept, and ignore also the inevitable criticism of our fellows, then originality may automatically reveal itself in our paintings. Artists, like writers, tell as much about themselves in their work as about their subjects.

There is no evidence to show that those who are most original ever said to themselves, "Now I'll be original." They never thought about originality. They just thought, and the results of their thinking were original because they themselves were different and they had the courage to say what they felt. Let me repeat, one cannot be original unless he has something of his own to say and the fortitude to say it. Real originality cannot be contrived.

EXPERIMENTATION

We should experiment continually. When we stop inquiring into new ways of seeing or doing, we are figuratively dead.

In testing new methods, however, no great change is required at any one step. It isn't necessary to develop an entirely new style every week. Change must be gradual — evolution, no revolution! Begin, perhaps, by using brushes of a different size and shape, or work with smooth paper instead of rough. Try casein for a while in place of transparent watercolor, then work out a combination of casein and aquarelle in the same painting. Alternate pictures made with broad loose washes with tightly detailed work. Many compositions may emerge as failures, but there should be progress in the long run.

VARIETY IN SUBJECT MATTER

We are all inclined to see only that which we want to see. If we like a certain type of subject, we will pass by other potentially interesting material without even seeing it and select repeatedly the kind of subjects that compose most easily for us. Many artists are painting today the same scenes that they were painting twenty years ago, and they are painting them in the same way. True, this adherence to "signature" is often demanded by sales agents, for many buyers will purchase only the kind of compositions that have given prominence to a painter. The practice may be profitable, but it is certainly fatal to artistic progress.

The habit of following the same scale pattern regularly should also be broken. If we tend to work always from a panorama viewpoint, we should occasionally shift to a close-up. Sometimes a house or other object that might be uninteresting in its entirety provides a successful composition when only a section or an attractive detail is featured. Impressive pictures have been painted from nothing more than an old wooden door. On the other hand, a panoramic view of a whole city may also be successful. The combinations of objects, large or small, impressive or common, many or few, that can make a good picture are limitless.

One good way to avoid getting in a rut regarding subject matter is to sketch outdoors regularly with other artists, allowing them to choose the subjects. At first you may see nothing desirable in the scenes chosen, but look for the qualities that attracted your fellow brush-wielders. This can open up whole new classes of picture material that might otherwise escape you. Often I have been amazed at the fine compositions extracted from material that to me seemed completely devoid of appeal.

POSITIVE AND NEGATIVE APPROACHES

Some artists claim they are able to compose a complete picture mentally before touching pencil or brush to paper, and that they can paint such pictures without hesitation and without trial sketches. That might be called the positive approach.

I must confess that I, for one, cannot duplicate such a performance and I doubt that many could. Mine is a more negative system. It might be called "correctional." Its point is to get *something* down on paper, then see what that calls for in the way of development or correction. I do have a general idea of what I want to do in advance, but I find that the composition on paper usually differs from the one imagined. Although I usually start with a very small sketch, as mentioned before, sometimes I work out the pattern in full size as the picture progresses. Once the main interest has been set down, experience permits one to proceed quickly, choosing and adding other features so easily an observer might believe the whole design to be preconceived.

Getting something on the paper is important. A visible pattern is much easier to evaluate than a mental image, and it can help in two ways. You can see promptly those things that are good and retain them. Those that are not good will often suggest their own remedy.

Mrs. Whitaker (the Eileen Monaghan whose paintings are reproduced on page 73) follows a kind of probing routine. Often an idea comes to her with an irresistible urge to get to work and develop it. Dropping everything, she concentrates and paints for many hours, adding and subtracting, brushing in and swabbing out until she is satisfied that the pattern is completely established. Then, and not until then, does she rest, for she finds that the inspiration subsides and the picture languishes if she relaxes earlier. Completion of the picture is almost a routine matter that can be taken up when convenient.

See "Blue Door" and "Fruit Still Life", page 73.

There is a good lesson in this, incidentally. When inspiration strikes, don't ignore it. Make as complete a record of it as possible. If time is limited, write out a memo at least.

COPYING THE WORK OF OTHERS

At one time it was common practice to copy the work of others as an aid to learning to paint. The idea is now widely frowned on. However, there is no legitimate reason why we should not imitate our betters. Whether we like to admit it or not, there is no such thing as completely creative thought or production. All new thoughts and new accomplishments stem in some way from earlier happenings. The more we know of the past the better we are able to contribute to the future.

In the old days, art was taught by the master to the pupil through enforced imitation. The apprentices became facsimile copies of the leader. Together they formed a school. Later these apprentices, after absorbing ideas from widely varying sources, became creators of schools of their own. Regardless of the imagined disadvantage of direct copying, no one can deny that in actual development of real artists, the apprentice system produced more and better results than our present scholastic system. It is a long time since we have had a Leonardo, a Michelangelo, and a Raphael producing at one time.

If a student wishes to copy the work of a master for practice, he may learn in a few minutes the reasons for procedures that it might require months to learn by fumbling and guessing. But when he has learned all his instructor has to offer, he should seek elsewhere for inspiration. To be a slave to any one idol can become dangerous. An artist should absorb the best of everything he sees.

PAINTING FROM PHOTOGRAPHS

Some artists have an idea that it is unethical to paint watercolors from photographs. However, a photograph represents nothing more than a record of an actual scene. If the artist exercises the same care in composing his painting from a photo that he would have used if painting from the subject itself, the finished painting should be equally acceptable. If you wish to save time by working from photos, you are certainly justified in so doing, at least occasionally. But you should not copy the photo any more than you would copy the original scene. Both should be used only as a basis for the painting. The painting "Village Fountain" was based on a photograph (Figure 56).

EYE VERSUS CAMERA

Few of us realize how our eyes interpret a scene. We do not see it as a camera does. A camera stares in one direction and records each picture detail according to the amount of light playing upon it. But looking at the same scene we see hundreds of individual "shots." We may look first at one detail, then gaze about, our eyes looking from spot to spot, until we have covered the entire expanse. We can see sharply only that spot upon which both eyes are focused — and that area is a very small one. Things seen out of the corner of the eye are quite vague. Hence the necessity for a roving eye.

The shutter of our eye (the iris) expands and contracts according to the amount of light it must accommodate, and it responds so easily and quickly as our gaze flits from lighted to shaded areas that we ourselves do not even realize it is operating. As it changes we are able to see detail in a cellar as clearly as in a sunlit field, though the former may have only one one-hundredth the illumination of the latter. So, as our gaze moves about the landscape, we see all details, light and dark, with equal clarity, not relatively as the camera does and as we must do when we paint a picture. Seeing in the manner described, we are prone to paint all details in the same key.

A picture cannot be painted as a combination of a hundred glances. It must be painted as a whole, with each area properly related to all other areas.

Because of the visual faculty described, one may see as very important a detail that is actually inconsequential when related to the whole scene.

The essence of sunlight, from a pictorial viewpoint, is contrast — strong contrast between the lights and the shadows. In painting, one can include in both light and shadow all the detail he desires, but he must remember that detail added to the light region makes it darker, while detail inserted in the dark shadow tends to lighten it, so the degree of contrast is reduced. The more detail, the less sunny brilliance, so one must use the mind as well as the eye to strike a satisfactory compromise.

Figure 56. Photograph of actual village fountain.

VILLAGE FOUNTAIN

13. DO'S AND DON'TS OF EXHIBITING

Many painters, especially those in artistically isolated communities, would like to exhibit their work but don't know how to go about it. Others send their work to open exhibitions around the country, paying expensive entry fees, to say nothing of the costs of crating and shipping, only to have their paintings repeatedly rejected. It is hoped that the suggestions in this section may help both groups.

LOCAL ART SOCIETIES

One of the best ways to learn the ins and outs of exhibiting is to join a local art society. You will be invited to participate in local exhibitions and will learn the routine of picture submission. From fellow members you will also hear about other exhibitions to which you can submit. If there is no existing art association in your neighborhood, organize one. A very small group of artists will suffice for a start, and you can learn from each other.

OTHER EXHIBITIONS

Even if there is no local art group for you to join, you can always subscribe to one of the art magazines that carry a calendar of coming exhibitions throughout the country. Choose the art shows that interest you and write for their explanatory prospectuses.

Some exhibitions are for the amateur, others for the regional professional, still others for nationally known artists. You must decide for yourself or learn, perhaps by painful and expensive experience, which class you belong in. If you are an amateur, you can save yourself disappointment and money by exhibiting only in that class until your work has really advanced. The judgment of juries is much more severe than that of personal friends. True, a beginner's work is sometimes accepted in an important exhibition by happy accident, and many think theirs will be such a miracle picture, but the chance is very slight.

THINGS TO AVOID

The kind of picture you send and the way you present it is important in competitive exhibitions. If you advertise your carelessness by submitting work in poor, jerry-built frames, with the backs falling out, you cannot

WINTER POSIES. 19¼″ x 13″

UPSTATE BRIDGE

VICTORIAN RELIC

HOME IN THE VALLEY

IN THE SHADOW OF THE HILLS

reasonably expect your work to be taken seriously. There are certain things that jurors seem instinctively and universally to dislike: outlandish frames, colored mats, "postcard blue" skies, superclever arrangements of any kind, illustrated jokes, thin wishy-washy effects, copies of other pictures, paintings palpably produced under a teacher's coaching, propaganda in any form, and saccharine sentimentalism. Of all qualities that arouse the resentment of art juries and critics, sugariness undoubtedly heads the list. This suspicion of any subject matter that is inherently charming may be psychological, but it does constitute a real hurdle for the painter. A very competent artist is needed to paint a non-saccharine picture of a naturally saccharine subject. It can be done but it isn't easy.

MATTING AND FRAMING WATERCOLORS

Pictures are framed either for use in the home or for entry in competitive exhibitions. A picture to be hung in the home is likely to be enclosed in a frame that not only suits the painting but also harmonizes with the decor of the room. The frame is usually "correct," neat and well-finished.

A painting for an art exhibition, on the other hand, must compete with perhaps hundreds of others in close packed arrangement. The function of the frame is that of a foil to show off the painting itself. If all entries were shown in assertive frames, the exhibition would be a riot; if only a few were submitted in gaudy frames, they would undoubtedly be hung in isolated and unfavorable spots. Art exhibition frames will usually hang well in the home, but the reverse is not always true. The following comments, therefore, refer primarily to framing pictures for exhibitions.

Most watercolors need a border of white, or near white, to set them off. Very few aquarelles can stand close framing like oils. Their character is less robust, so ½" to 5" mats are usually placed between the picture and the frame. The 4" or 5" white mats with ½" or ¾" frames that were popular for many years are now seldom seen in national exhibitions, though they are still popular in regional shows. It is better to use 1¾" frames with such mats.

Many commercial art galleries prefer that watercolors be matted only, because frames take up too much rack space. Most exhibiting societies now accept unframed watercolors mounted in white mats from distant artists. The unframed, matted pictures are shown under sheets of glass. For this purpose, substantial mats are required. They should measure about 4" in width and, if made of thin mat board, should be backed with other boards for strength.

When attaching pictures to the backs of mats, avoid the use of masking tape or cellophane tape, for the holding power of either is of brief duration. Don't tape the pictures on all four edges or the paper will buckle when it expands due to humidity. Fasten only at the top, with strong adhesive paper, and let the picture hang free, held in place by its backing. This will allow for expansion and contraction.

A good backing for a substantial mat (to be used without a frame) can be made by cutting a piece of corrugated paperboard which is 1" less all around than the mat itself, and sticking it around the edges with gummed

UNION SQUARE

The arrangement and sizes of the many figures in this scene were calculated as described on page 84. Notice that, for interest only, a few of the figures have been treated as individuals while the others are simply group details. The architecture is broadly painted, with details merely suggested. The pavement, made up of hexagonal tiles, was accurately and mechanically laid out under the rules of linear perspective and then substantially "lost" to provide an artistic appearance. The sky, not at all naturalistic, is painted in gray and cream, with a mass of individual brush strokes.

paper. This combination will stand a good deal of handling. If the mat becomes scuffed it can be repainted or retouched with white casein paint.

A duotone mat — white and gray — is an attractive and popular frame for a watercolor. For a 22″ x 30″ painting use a white mat 1⅛″ wide. Outside that place a medium gray mat 3¼″ wide, allowing an extra margin to go into the frame rabbet. A simple wood frame, 2″ wide, with a gray-brown finish, looks well with this. These outside dimensions of both the white and gray mats can be the same. Just cut the aperture in the gray mat 2¼″ larger in length and width than the white one and cement the two together near the inside edge of the gray one. Both mats may be of regular mat board, but the best double mats are made with 3/16″ wallboard for the inner mat and regular 1/16″ mat board for the outer mat. The mats and frames for smaller pictures can be reduced in width relatively.

The white inside–gray outside arrangement is good for paintings that are fairly strong in color. For pictures that contain a great deal of white space, especially around the edges, reverse the pattern, making the inner mat gray and the outer mat white. Beware of colored mats. They compete too forcefully with the picture and will almost certainly insure rejection by juries.

Now a word about frames. For exhibition purposes, wormy chestnut, stained in various shades from gray to brown (depending on whether the picture needs a warm or cool toned frame) is extremely popular today. Any other wood is acceptable if properly toned. Remember that a wide frame should usually have a narrow mat, and a relatively narrow frame a wide mat. Don't combine a wide mat and a wide frame.

If color is used on the wood (as in carved and tinted frames) be sure it is muted and uninsistent. The color on the frame should approximate at least one of the picture hues. White, black, gray, or metallic gold (but not yellow) will harmonize with any color.

The width of the frame in relation to the mats, its color or warmth in relation to the picture colors, and the scale of the frame and mat in relation to the scale and key of the painting are the important factors to consider. A delicate picture should not be shown in a bold frame nor a strong picture in a weak one. The function of the frame is to show off the picture. It must complement the picture, but not dominate it.

HOW TO MAKE MATS

The most serviceable mats are made of a 3/16″ wallboard such as beaver board. This is a pulpboard procurable from any lumber yard. The standard size is 4′ x 8′, though there are other sizes. Regular mat board of ⅛″ or 1/16″ thickness comes in 30″ x 40″ sheets.

Mat cutting requires a metal straightedge and a very sharp cutting tool. Razor blades in patented handles will serve, but the blade's flexibility can produce curved cuts if you are not careful. I prefer either the Stanley or Speedy trimming knife, available in hardware, art supply, and stationery stores. These have metal or plastic handles and double-edged removable blades, which are as sharp as razor blades but considerably thicker. The straightedge must be of metal; otherwise the knife will cut slices from it.

The card should be cut on a firm flat surface, hard enough to permit the cutting of a clean edge and soft enough not to dull the knife point. To protect your table, you can place a loose strip of cardboard under the mat being cut.

Now for the cutting. First cut the board to fit the outside dimensions desired. You are now ready to cut the inner edges. This is the operation that troubles most mat makers, for the cuts must be beveled, and they must be clean and even. Remember that the pebbled surface is the face of the board and the smooth surface is the back. With a pencil, mark lightly the size of the desired aperture, allowing ⅜″ or ½″ on each of the four sides to cover the edge of the painting. Next lay the metal straightedge on the board about 1/16″ *outside* the pencil lines. Hold it firmly in place with the left hand, then take the trimming knife in the right hand and draw it lightly along the metal straightedge, from one corner of the pencilled rectangle to the other. Slant the blade at a sixty degree angle so that, when the bevel is finished, the inside edge will be directly under the original pencil line. Do not press the knife too hard, especially on the first two or three draws, or you may force the straightedge out of place and cut a wavy line. When the incision has been definitely established, you may discard the straightedge and, holding the card so the knife may be drawn toward you, finish the cutting with a number of fairly light strokes. This will leave a perfect bevel with clean edges front and back. Repeat the process on the other three sides. Be sure that the incisions extend well into the corners, for these points have a tendency to hold and cause a ragged effect. Change the blades when they begin to drag. It is impossible to cut a good mat with anything less than a very sharp blade. If by chance the back edge of the bevel is fuzzy, smooth it with sandpaper on a small wooden block. With practice, you can cut good mats very quickly.

Most wallboards are gray or cream colored, so they must be painted. Use a brush or sprayer and a commercial casein paint which comes in quart cans. You can set it in either warm or cold white. It mixes with water but, once dry, is no longer soluble. I prefer to use two coats, both quite thin. The first simply seals the pores of the board and the second provides the opacity. The second coat can be applied an hour or two after the first, but the second should stand a day or two until all moisture has evaporated. For thinner mats than wallboard, no painting is required.

GLASS REFLECTIONS

Some people dislike the idea of watercolors framed under glass because the glass picks up reflections. They wonder why pictures can't be shown without glass or with a non-reflecting glass.

I am against the use of non-reflecting glass because it takes all the life out of a painting and makes it resemble a print. Many artists have tried it, but all I have known rejected it later. Watercolor needs the brilliance of glass to give sparkle and density to the colors. Any objectionable reflection can usually be overcome by changing the pitch of the picture in relation to the wall.

As for exhibiting a good watercolor for any great length of time without glass protection, I feel it borders on desecration. The picture will eventually become filthy, and it cannot be restored. Watercolors cannot be cleaned like oils.

KEEP A RECORD OF YOUR PAINTINGS

Once you start exhibiting your work, you will need a simple system for recording the whereabouts of your paintings. It can save you the embarrassment, for instance, of sending the same picture twice to the same society. It may also save a number of pictures, for those unrecorded have a disturbing tendency to become lost.

Standard 5″ x 8″ ruled file cards are excellent for the purpose. Figure 57 shows my system. Each card contains the title of one painting, a brief description of it for identification, whither and when it was sent, the price quoted, when it was returned, and its final disposition. Cards are filed in alphabetical order.

For my own convenience I also use three standard correspondence filing folders marked, respectively, "Coming Exhibitions," "Pictures on Exhibit," and "Returned from Exhibitions." These hold prospectuses of exhibits. I receive many such prospectuses each year. When one arrives I underline on it the date for picture delivery, write that and the name of the society in a one-line memo on the front of the "Coming Exhibitions" folder, and drop the prospectus in the folder. As pictures are delivered to exhibitions, the memos are crossed out, and the names and prices of the pictures sent are noted on the prospectus, which is transferred to the "Pictures on Exhibit" folder. At the appropriate time, the prospectus is transferred to the "Returned" folder. This system gives me a complete record of the picture's history, its present location, expected date of return, and actual date of return.

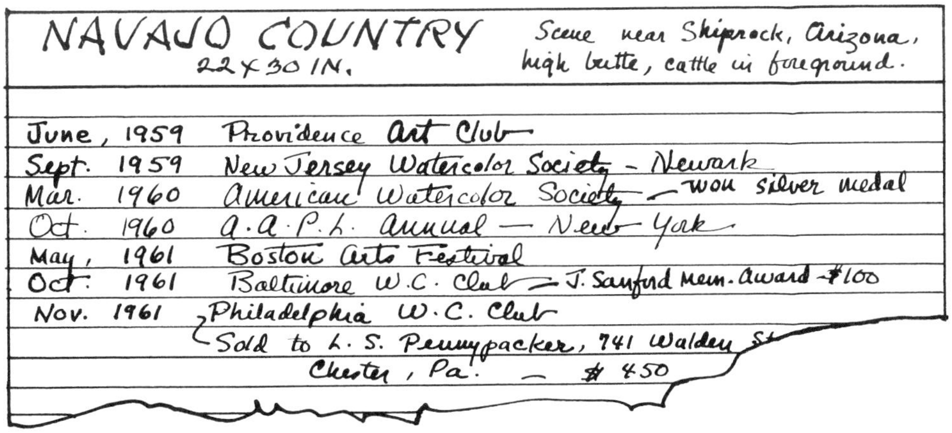
NAVAJO COUNTRY — Scene near Shiprock, Arizona, high butte, cattle in foreground.
22 x 30 IN.

June, 1959	Providence Art Club	
Sept. 1959	New Jersey Watercolor Society - Newark	
Mar. 1960	American Watercolor Society	won silver medal
Oct. 1960	A.A.P.L. Annual — New York	
May, 1961	Boston Arts Festival	
Oct. 1961	Baltimore W.C. Club	J. Sanford Mem. Award $100
Nov. 1961	Philadelphia W.C. Club	
	Sold to L. S. Pennypacker, 741 Walden St. Chester, Pa. — $450	

Figure 57. Standard file cards, 5 x 8 inches, can be used to keep track of your paintings when you send them out to exhibitions.

14. A BRIEF HISTORY OF WATERCOLOR

Transparent watercolor as we know it was developed in England toward the end of the eighteenth century. The nearest approach to it before that time was a method of sketching in ink and tinting the drawing with watercolor.

In the eighteenth century, an English painter named Paul Sandby (1725–1809) worked out a technique of straight watercolor painting, without ink, which was carried on by Alexander Cozens (d. 1786) and his son John R. Cozens (1752–1797) and perfected by Thomas Girtin (1775–1802).

The new method was called aquarelle. No opaque color was used, the lights being achieved by thinning the pigment with water. This technique is the one generally followed throughout the British Commonwealth to this day. American watercolor, until recently at least, has followed the British approach. In other European countries, watercolor developed in a somewhat different manner. In France, for instance, gouache became the accepted form and relatively little transparent work has been produced.

Sandby and his followers were the precursors of a talented British school, among whom Joseph M. W. Turner (1775–1851) was the leading light. His work demonstrated the full capacity of the medium. He was an early student of Cozens' painting and he worked with Girtin until the latter's untimely death. Turner's early pictures were low in tone and gloomy, though forcible and convincing. His best were his Venetian aquarelles, painted on the spot. Occasionally he used gouache or pastel with the watercolor, or accented his work with pencil or pen. He never revealed to anyone the secrets of his technique — a technique which, combined with his great artistic intellect, made him, in the opinion of many, the greatest watercolor landscapist the world has known.

In 1804 the Old Water Colour Society was founded. It later became the Royal Society of Painters in Water Colour. The Royal Institute of Painters in Water Colour was established in 1831. These organizations gave great impulse to the art. Among the greatest watercolorists of the early school were Copley Fielding (d. 1855), Richard Bonington (d. 1828), John Cotman (d. 1842), Peter De Wint (d. 1849), Samuel Prout (d. 1852),

David Cox, master of architectural painting (d. 1859), and J. F. Lewis (d. 1876), known for his Oriental genre paintings.

Bonington died at twenty-six, but he exerted a strong influence on early British watercolors and it is claimed that he was the first to show the French the possibilities of the medium. While studying in Paris, he became friendly with Isabey and Delacroix, who was one of the first to sense the genius of the Englishman. It is said that a painting by Bonington in a Paris window inspired Corot to take up painting.

In the 19th century, two great English painters of animals, Sir Edwin Landseer (d. 1873), and G. L. Taylor (d. 1873), achieved notable success in the field of aquarelle. Other eminent British watercolorists of the period were George Cattermole (d. 1868), F. Walker (d. 1875), Sir John Gilbert (d. 1897) and the Pre-Raphaelites, Dante Gabriel Rossetti (d. 1882), Ford Madox Brown (d. 1893), Sir Edward Burne-Jones (d. 1898), W. Holman Hunt (d. 1910), and Sir John Everett Millais (d. 1896). British aquarellists of the early 20th century included Alfred East, Sir W. Russell Flint, Arthur Rackham, Arthur Wardle, Lamorna Birch, Frank Brangwyn, and Dame Laura Knight.

Watercolor reached its heights in France with the Oriental sketches of Eugene Delacroix (1798–1863). Guillaume Descamps (1803–1860) was one of the best colorists and most original painters of the mid-century French school, and Gavarni (1804–1866) produced powerful genres that created a sensation even among the reserved Britishers. Other outstanding exponents of watercolor in France were I. B. Isabey, J. B. L. Hubert, J. Ouvrie, Eugene Sué, Simeon Fort, and Pierre J. Redouté. Redouté was considered the best painter of flowers in watercolor that France has produced.

The practice of watercolor painting spread over all the world during the 19th century, though never with such outstanding results as in the English- and French-speaking countries. Today, of course, with our more closely knit world, the painting of watercolors is well-nigh universally followed.

We have intentionally spoken at some length on British watercolorists, for the best American watercolor is based firmly upon British method and outlook. The practice of aquarelle was quickly translated to this country after its British inception and has been an important aspect of American art. Thomas Cole, Asher Brown Durand, and other members of the 19th century Hudson River School executed gems of watercolor after the style of the best masters. Among the early great painters of the West, Albert Bierstadt and Thomas Moran were outstanding watercolorists.

Undoubtedly Winslow Homer has influenced American watercolor more than any other individual. Great as has been his reputation in oil, many consider his watercolors his finest contribution to art. Certainly they left an impress that, directly or indirectly, has influenced every American watercolorist since his time.

Homer was an early member of the American Watercolor Society, which will celebrate the centennial of its founding in 1966. This organization was patterned after the Royal Water Colour Society and has been of inestimable value to American art. Its purpose is to foster the advancement of watercolor painting, and it does this in a variety of useful ways.

Many of the great names in American watercolor since the Civil War have been members of the American Watercolor Society. Students should be familiar with the work of such men as Edwin A. Abbey, Frank W. Benson, E. H. Blashfield, Robert Blum, William Chase, Charles De Muth, Gordon Grant, George (Pop) Hart, Childe Hassam, Winslow Homer, Theodore Kautzky, John La Farge, Thomas Moran, J. Francis Murphy, Charles Parsons, Maurice Prendergast, Edward Penfield, H. W. Ranger, Chauncy Ryder, John Singer Sargent, Everett Shinn, R. M. Shurtleff, F. Hopkinson Smith, Louis C. Tiffany, J. Alden Weir, Irving R. Wiles, Alex H. Wyant, and James McNeill Whistler.

MEXICAN MEMORIAL